CAHSEE Review!

Complete CAHSEE Study Guide and Practice Test Questions

Published by

Blue Butterfly Books™

Copyright © 2013, by *Blue Butterfly Books*™, Sheila M. Hynes. ALL RIGHTS RESERVED. No part of this book may be reproduced or transferred in any form or by any means, graphic, electronic, or mechanical, including photocopying, recording, web distribution, taping, or by any information storage retrieval system, without the written permission of the author.

Notice: *Blue Butterfly Books*™ makes every reasonable effort to obtain from reliable sources accurate, complete, and timely information about the tests covered in this book. Nevertheless, changes can be made in the tests or the administration of the tests at any time and *Blue Butterfly Books* ™ makes no representation or warranty, either expressed or implied as to the accuracy, timeliness, or completeness of the information contained in this book. *Blue Butterfly Books* ™ makes no representations or warranties of any kind, express or implied, about the completeness, accuracy, reliability, suitability or availability with respect to the information contained in this document for any purpose. Any reliance you place on such information is therefore strictly at your own risk.

The author(s) shall not be liable for any loss incurred as a consequence of the use and application, directly or indirectly, of any information presented in this work. Sold with the understanding, the author is not engaged in rendering professional services or advice. If advice or expert assistance is required, the services of a competent professional should be sought.

The company, product and service names used in this book are for identification purposes only. All trademarks and registered trademarks are the property of their respective owners. *Blue Butterfly Books* ™ is not affiliate with any educational institution.

We strongly recommend that students check with exam providers for up-to-date information regarding test content.

The CAHSEE Exam is administered by the California Department of Education, who are not involved in the production of, and do not endorse this publication.

Published by

Blue Butterfly Books™
Victoria BC Canada

Printed in the USA

Version 6.5 March 2015

Team Members for this publication

Editor: Brian Stocker MA
Contributor: Dr. C. Gregory
Contributor: Dr. G. A. Stocker DDS
Contributor: D. A. Stocker M. Ed.
Contributor: Sheila M. Hynes, MES York, BA (Hons)
Contributor: Elizabeta Petrovic MSc (Mathematics)
Contributor: Kelley O'Malley BA (English)

Sustainability and Eco-Responsibility

Here at *Blue Butterfly Books*™, trees are valuable to Mother Earth and the health and wellbeing of everyone. Minimizing our ecological footprint and effect on the environment, we choose Create Space, an eco-responsible printing company.

Electronic routing of our books reduces greenhouse gas emissions, worldwide. When a book order is received, the order is filled at the printing location closest to the client. Using environmentally friendly publishing technology, of the Espresso book printing machine, *Blue Butterfly Books*™ are printed as they are requested, saving thousands of books, and trees over time. This process offers the stable and viable alternative keeping healthy sustainability of our environment.

All paper is acid-free, and interior paper stock is made from 30% post-consumer waste recycled material. Safe for children, Create Space also verifies the materials used in the print process are all CPSIA-compliant.

By purchasing this *Blue Butterfly Books*™, you have supported Full Recovery and Preservation of The Karner Blue Butterfly. Our logo is the Karner Blue Butterfly, Lycaeides melissa samuelis, a rare and beautiful butterfly species whose only flower for propogation is the blue lupin flower. The Karner Butterfly is mostly found in the Great Lakes Region of the U.S.A. Recovery planning is in action, for the return of Karner Blue in Canada led by the National Recovery Strategy. The recovery goals and objectives are aimed at recreating suitable habitats for the butterfly and encourage the growth of blue lupines - the butterfly's natural ideal habitat.

For more info on the Karner Blue Butterfly , feel free to visit:

http://www.albanypinebush.org/conservation/wildlife-management/karner-blue-butterfly-recovery

http://www.wiltonpreserve.org/conservation/karner-blue-butterfly.

http://www.natureconservancy.ca/en/what-we-do/resource-centre/featured-species/karner_blue.html.

Contents

8 **Getting Started**
How this study guide is organized 9
The CAHSEE Study Plan 10
Making a Study Schedule 10

16 **Reading**
Self-Assessment 17
Answer Key 27
Help with Reading Comprehension 29
Main Idea and Supporting Details 32
Drawing Inferences And Conclusions 36

40 **Mathematics**
Self-Assessment 44
Answer Key 58
Fraction Tips, Tricks and Shortcuts 67
Decimal Tips, Tricks and Shortcuts 68
Percent Tips, Tricks and Shortcuts 72
Mean, Median and Mode 76
Basic Math Multiple Choice 78
How to Solve Word Problems 82
Types of Word Problems 85
Order of Operation 93
Scientific Notation 94
Ratios 96
Cartesian and Coordinate Plane 100
Pythagorean Geometry 105
Congruence 107
Quadrilaterals 111
One-Variable Linear Equations 113
Two-Variable Linear Equations 114

116 **English Language Arts**
Self-Assessment 119
Answer Key 127
English Tutorials 130
Capitalization 130
Punctuation 132

	Hyphens	133
	Apostrophes	135
	Commas	136
	Quotation Marks	138
	Common English Usage Mistakes	139
	Subject Verb Agreement	146
	Essay Revision Self-Assessment	153
	Answer Key	160
163	**How to Write an Essay**	
	Formulating A Thesis	173
	Common Essay Mistakes - 1	176
	Common Essay Mistakes - 2	178
	Writing Concisely	180
	Redundancy	182
190	**Practice Test Questions Set 1**	
	Answer Key	238
258	**Practice Test Questions Set 2**	
	Answer Key	304
323	**Conclusion**	

Getting Started

CONGRATULATIONS! By deciding to take the California High School Exit Exam (CAHSEE), you have taken the first step toward a great future! Of course, there is no point in taking this important examination unless you intend to do your very best to earn the highest grade you possibly can. That means getting yourself organized and discovering the best approaches, methods and strategies to master the material. Yes, that will require real effort and dedication on your part but if you are willing to focus your energy and devote the study time necessary, before you know it you will be on you way to a brighter future!

We know that taking on a new endeavour can be a little scary, and it is easy to feel unsure of where to begin. That's where we come in. This study guide is designed to help you improve your test-taking skills, show you a few tricks of the trade and increase both your competency and confidence.

The California High School Exit Exam

The CAHSEE exam is composed of three modules, reading, mathematics and writing. The reading section consists of reading comprehension questions and vocabulary. The mathematics section contains basic math, algebra, geometry and problem solving. The writing section contains an essay question, English grammar and usage multiple choice, and essay revision questions.

While we seek to make our guide as comprehensive as possible, note that like all exams, the CAHSEE Exam might be adjusted at some future point. New material might be added, or content that is no longer relevant or applicable might be removed. It is always a good idea to give the materials you receive when you register to take the CAHSEE a careful review.

How this study guide is organized

This study guide is divided into three sections. The first section, Self-Assessments, which will help you recognize your areas of strength and weaknesses. This will be a boon when it comes to managing your study time most efficiently; there is not much point of focusing on material you have already got firmly under control. Instead, taking the self-assessments will show you where that time could be much better spent. In this area you will begin with a few questions to quickly evaluate your understanding of material that is likely to appear on the CAHSEE. If you do poorly in certain areas, simply work carefully through those sections in the tutorials and then try the self-assessment again.

The second section, Tutorials, offers information in each of the content areas, as well as strategies to help you master that material. The tutorials are not intended to be a complete course, but cover general principals. If you find that you do not understand the tutorials, it is recommended that you seek out additional instruction.

Third, we offer two sets of practice test questions, similar to those on the CAHSEE Exam.

The CAHSEE Study Plan

Now that you have made the decision to take the CAHSEE, it is time to get started. Before you do another thing, you will need to figure out a plan of attack. The very best study tip is to start early! The longer the time period you devote to regular study practice, the more likely you will be to retain the material and be able to access it quickly. If you thought that 1x20 is the same as 2x10, guess what? It really is not, when it comes to study time. Reviewing material for just an hour per day over the course of 20 days is far better than studying for two hours a day for only 10 days. The more often you revisit a particular piece of information, the better you will know it. Not only will your grasp and understanding be better, but your ability to reach into your brain and quickly and efficiently pull out the tidbit you need, will be greatly enhanced as well.

The great Chinese scholar and philosopher Confucius believed that true knowledge could be defined as knowing both what you know and what you do not know. The first step in preparing for the CAHSEE is to assess your strengths and weaknesses. You may already have an idea of what you know and what you do not know, but evaluating yourself using our Self- Assessment modules for each of the three areas, Math, Writing and Reading Comprehension, will clarify the details.

Making a Study Schedule

To make your study time most productive you will need to develop a study plan. The purpose of the plan is to organize all the bits of pieces of information in such a way that you will not feel overwhelmed. Rome was not built in a day, and learning everything you will need to know to pass the CAHSEE is going to take time, too. Arranging the material you need to learn into manageable chunks is the best way to go. Each study session should make you feel as though you have succeeded in accomplishing your goal, and your goal is simply to learn what you planned to learn during that particular session. Try to organize the content in such a way that each study session builds upon previous ones. That way, you will retain the information, be better able to access it, and review the previous bits and pieces at the same time.

Self-assessment

The Best Study Tip! The very best study tip is to start early! The longer you study regularly, the more you will retain and 'learn' the material. Studying for 1 hour per day for 20 days is far better than studying for 2 hours for 10 days.

What don't you know?

The first step is to assess your strengths and weaknesses. You may already have an idea of where your weaknesses are, or you can take our Self-assessment modules for each of the areas CAHSEE content areas.

Exam Component	Rate from 1 to 5
Reading Comprehension	
Vocabulary (Meaning in Context)	
Main idea	
Mathematics	
Decimals Percent and Fractions	
Interpreting Graphs and Tables	
Mean, mode and median	
Basic Algebra	
Geometry	
Problem Solving	

Writing	
Essay writing	
Sentence structure & usage	

Making a Study Schedule

The key to making a study plan is to divide the material you need to learn into manageable size and learn it, while at the same time reviewing the material that you already know.

Using the table above, any scores of three or below, you need to spend time learning, going over and practicing this subject area. A score of four means you need to review the material, but you don't have to spend time re-learning. A score of five and you are OK with just an occasional review before the exam.

A score of zero or one means you really do need to work on this and you should allocate the most time and give it the highest priority. Some students prefer a 5-day plan and others a 10-day plan. It also depends on how much time you have until the exam.

Here is an example of a 5-day plan based on an example from the table above:

Main Idea: 1   Study 1 hour everyday – review on last day
Fractions: 3   Study 1 hour for 2 days then ½ hour and then review
Algebra: 4   Review every second day
Grammar & Usage: 2 Study 1 hour on the first day – then ½ hour everyday
Reading Comprehension: 5   Review for ½ hour every other day
Geometry: 5 Review for ½ hour every other day

Using this example, geometry and reading comprehension

are good and only need occasional review. Algebra is good and needs 'some' review. Fractions need a bit of work, grammar and usage needs a lot of work and Main Idea is very weak and need the majority of time. Based on this, here is a sample study plan:

Day	Subject	Time
Monday		
Study	Main Idea	1 hour
Study	Grammar & Usage	1 hour
	½ hour break	
Study	Fractions	1 hour
Review	Algebra	½ hour
Tuesday		
Study	Main Idea	1 hour
Study	Grammar & Usage	½ hour
	½ hour break	
Study	Fractions	½ hour
Review	Algebra	½ hour
Review	Geometry	½ hour
Wednesday		
Study	Main Idea	1 hour
Study	Grammar & Usage	½ hour
	½ hour break	
Study	Fractions	½ hour
Review	Geometry	½ hour
Thursday		
Study	Main Idea	½ hour
Study	Grammar & Usage	½ hour
Review	Fractions	½ hour
	½ hour break	
Review	Geometry	½ hour
Review	Algebra	½ hour
Friday		
Review	Main Idea	½ hour
Review	Grammar & Usage	½ hour

Review	Fractions	½ hour
	½ hour break	
Review	Algebra	½ hour
Review	Grammar & Usage	½ hour

Using this example, adapt the study plan to your own schedule. This schedule assumes 2 ½ - 3 hours available to study everyday for a 5 day period.

First, write out what you need to study and how much. Next figure out how many days you have before the test. Note, do NOT study on the last day before the test. On the last day before the test, you won't learn anything and will probably only confuse yourself.

Make a table with the days before the test and the number of hours you have available to study each day. We suggest working with 1 hour and ½ hour time slots.

Start filling in the blanks, with the subjects you need to study the most getting the most time and the most regular time slots (i.e. everyday) and the subjects that you know getting the least time (e.g. ½ hour every other day, or every 3rd day).

Tips for making a schedule

Once you make a schedule, stick with it! Make your study sessions reasonable. If you make a study schedule and don't stick with it, you set yourself up for failure. Instead, schedule study sessions that are a bit shorter and set yourself up for success! Make sure your study sessions are do-able. Studying is hard work but after you pass, you can party and take a break!

Schedule breaks. Breaks are just as important as study time. Work out a rotation of studying and breaks that works for you.

Build up study time. If you find it hard to sit still and study for 1 hour straight through, build up to it. Start with 20 minutes, and then take a break. Once you get used to 20-minute study sessions, increase the time to 30 minutes.

Gradually work you way up to 1 hour.

40 minutes to 1 hour is optimal. Studying for longer than this is tiring and not productive. Studying for shorter isn't long enough to be productive.

Studying Math. Studying Math is different from studying other subjects because you use a different part of your brain. The best way to study math is to practice everyday. This will train your mind to think in a mathematical way. If you miss a day or days, the mathematical mind-set is gone and you have to start all over again to build it up.

Study and practice math everyday for at least 5 days before the exam.

Reading

THIS SECTION CONTAINS A SELF-ASSESSMENT AND READING TUTORIAL. The tutorials are designed to familiarize general principles and the self-assessment contains general questions similar to the reading questions likely to be on the CAHSEE, but are not intended to be identical to the exam questions. The tutorials are not designed to be a complete reading course, and it is assumed that students have some familiarity with reading comprehension questions. If you do not understand parts of the tutorial, or find the tutorial difficult, it is recommended that you seek out additional instruction.

Tour of the CAHSEE Reading Content

The CAHSEE reading section has 40 reading questions which include reading comprehension and vocabulary. Below is a more detailed list of the types of reading questions that generally appear on the CAHSEE. Make sure you understand all of these points at a very minimum.

- Drawing logical conclusions

- Identify the author's purpose to persuade, inform, entertain, or otherwise

- Make predictions

- Analyze and evaluate the use of text structure to solve problems or identify sequences

- Vocabulary - Give the definition of a word from context

- Summarize

The questions below are not the same as you will find on the CAHSEE - that would be too easy! And nobody knows what the questions will be and they change all the time. Mostly the changes consist of substituting new questions for old, but the changes can be new question formats or styles, changes to the number of questions in each section, changes to the time limits for each section and combining sections. Below are general reading questions that cover the same areas as the CAHSEE. So, while the format and exact wording of the questions may differ slightly, and change from year to year, if you can answer the questions below, you will have no problem with the reading section of the CAHSEE.

Reading Self-Assessment

The purpose of the self-assessment is:

- Identify your strengths and weaknesses.

- Develop your personalized study plan (above)

- Get accustomed to the CAHSEE format

- Extra practice – the self-assessments are almost a full 3rd practice test!

- Provide a baseline score for preparing your study

schedule.

Since this is a Self-assessment, and depending on how confident you are with Reading Comprehension, timing is optional. The CAHSEE has 40 reading questions. The self-assessment has 14 questions, so allow about 20 minutes to complete this assessment.

Once complete, use the table below to assess your understanding of the content, and prepare your study schedule described in chapter 1.

80% - 100%	Excellent – you have mastered the content
60 – 79%	Good. You have a working knowledge. Even though you can just pass this section, you may want to review the tutorials and do some extra practice to see if you can improve your mark.
40% - 59%	Below Average. You do not understand the reading comprehension problems. Review the tutorials, and retake this quiz again in a few days, before proceeding to the Practice Test Questions.
Less than 40%	Poor. You have a very limited understanding of the reading comprehension problems. Please review the tutorials, and retake this quiz again in a few days, before proceeding to the Practice Test Questions.

Reading Comprehension Self-Assessment Answer Sheet

1. (A) (B) (C) (D) 11. (A) (B) (C) (D)

2. (A) (B) (C) (D) 12. (A) (B) (C) (D)

3. (A) (B) (C) (D) 13. (A) (B) (C) (D)

4. (A) (B) (C) (D) 14. (A) (B) (C) (D)

5. (A) (B) (C) (D)

6. (A) (B) (C) (D)

7. (A) (B) (C) (D)

8. (A) (B) (C) (D)

9. (A) (B) (C) (D)

10. (A) (B) (C) (D)

Questions 1 – 4 refer to the following passage.

Passage 1 - The Immune System

An immune system is a system of biological structures and processes that protects against disease by identifying and killing pathogens and other threats. The immune system can detect a wide variety of agents, from viruses to parasitic worms, and distinguish them from the organism's own healthy cells and tissues. Detection is complicated as pathogens evolve rapidly to avoid the immune system defences, and successfully infect their hosts.

The human immune system consists of many types of proteins, cells, organs, and tissues, which interact in an elaborate and dynamic network. As part of this more complex immune response, the human immune system adapts over time to recognize specific pathogens more efficiently. This adaptation process is called "adaptive immunity" or "acquired immunity" and creates immunological memory. Immunological memory created from a primary response to a specific pathogen, provides an enhanced response to future encounters with that same pathogen. This process of acquired immunity is the basis of vaccination. [1]

1. What can we infer from the first paragraph in this passage?

    a. When a person's body fights off the flu, this is the immune system in action

    b. When a person's immune system functions correctly, they avoid all sicknesses and injuries

    c. When a person's immune system is weak, a person will likely get a terminal disease

    d. When a person's body fights off a cold, this is the circulatory system in action

2. The immune system's primary function is to:

    a. Strengthen the bones

    b. Protect against disease

    c. Improve respiration

    d. Improve circulation

3. Based on the passage, what can we say about evolution's role in the immune system?

    a. Evolution of the immune system is an important factor in the immune system's efficiency

    b. Evolution causes a person to die, thus killing the pathogen

    c. Evolution plays no known role in immunity

    d. The least evolved earth species have better immunity

4. Which sentence below, taken from the passage, tell us the main idea of the passage?

    a. The human immune system consists of many types of proteins, cells, organs, and tissues, which interact in an elaborate and dynamic network.

    b. An immune system is a system of biological structures and processes that protects against disease by identifying and killing pathogens and other threats.

    c. The immune system can detect a wide variety of agents, from viruses to parasitic worms, and distinguish them from the organism's own healthy cells and tissues.

    d. None of these express the main idea.

Questions 5 – 8 refer to the following passage.

Passage 2 - White Blood Cells

White blood cells (WBCs), or leukocytes (also spelled "leucocytes"), are cells of the immune system that defend the body against both infectious disease and foreign material. Five different and diverse types of leukocytes exist, but they are all produced and derived from a powerful cell in the bone marrow known as a hematopoietic stem cell. Leukocytes are found throughout the body, including the blood and lymphatic system.

The number of WBCs in the blood is often an indicator of disease. There are normally between 4×10^9 and 1.1×10^{10} white blood cells in a liter of blood, making up about 1% of blood in a healthy adult. The physical properties of white blood cells, such as volume, conductivity, and granularity, changes due to the presence of immature cells, or malignant cells.

The name white blood cell derives from the fact that after processing a blood sample in a centrifuge, the white cells are typically a thin, white layer of nucleated cells. The scientific term leukocyte directly reflects this description, derived from Greek leukos (white), and kytos (cell). [2]

5. What can we infer from the first paragraph in this selection?

    a. Red blood cells are not as important as white blood cells

    b. White blood cells are the culprits in most infectious diseases

    c. White blood cells are essential to fight off infectious diseases

    d. Red blood cells are essential to fight off infectious diseases

6. What can we say about the number of white blood cells in a liter of blood?

    a. They make up about 1% of a healthy adult's blood

    b. There are 10^{10} WBCs in a healthy adult's blood

    c. The number varies according to age

    d. They are a thin white layer of nucleated cells

7. What is a more scientific term for "white blood cell?"

    a. Red blood cell

    b. Anthrocyte

    c. Leukocyte

    d. Leukemia

8. Can the number of leukocytes indicate cancer?

    a. Yes, the white blood cell count can indicate disease.

    b. No, the white blood cell count is not a reliable indicator.

    c. Disease may indicate a high white blood cell count.

    d. None of the choices are correct.

Questions 9 – 12 refer to the following passage.

Keeping Tropical Fish

Keeping tropical fish at home or in your office used to be very popular. Today interest has declined, but it remains as rewarding and relaxing a hobby as ever. Ask any tropical fish hobbyist, and you will hear how soothing and relaxing watching colorful fish live their lives in the aquarium. If you are considering keeping tropical fish as pets, here is a list of the basic equipment you will need.

A filter is essential for keeping your aquarium clean and your fish alive and healthy. There are different types and sizes of filters and the right size for you depends on the size of the aquarium and the level of stocking. Generally, you need a filter with a 3 to 5 times turn over rate per hour. This means that the water in the tank should go through the filter about 3 to 5 times per hour.

Most tropical fish do well in water temperatures ranging between 24° C and 26° C, though each has its own ideal water temperature. A heater with a thermostat is necessary to regulate the water temperature. Some heaters are submersible and others are not, so check carefully before you buy.

Lights are also necessary, and come in a large variety of types, strengths and sizes. A light source is necessary for plants in the tank to photosynthesize and give the tank a more attractive appearance. Even if you plan to use plastic plants, the fish still require light, although here, you can use a lower strength light source.

A hood is necessary to keep dust, dirt and unwanted materials out of the tank. Sometimes the hood can also help prevent evaporation. Another requirement is aquarium gravel. This will help improve the aesthetics of the aquarium and is necessary if you plan to have real plants.

9. What is the general tone of this article?

    a. Formal

    b. Informal

    c. Technical

    d. Opinion

10. Which of the following can not be inferred?

    a. Gravel is good for aquarium plants.

    b. Fewer people have aquariums in their office than at home.

    c. The larger the tank, the larger the filter required.

    d. None of the above.

11. What evidence does the author provide to support their claim that aquarium lights are necessary?

    a. Plants require light.

    b. Fish and plants require light.

    c. The author does not provide evidence for this statement.

    d. Aquarium lights make the aquarium more attractive.

12. Which of the following is an opinion?

    a. Filter with a 3 to 5 times turn over rate per hour are required.

    b. Aquarium gravel improves the aesthetics of the aquarium.

    c. An aquarium hood keeps dust, dirt and unwanted materials out of the tank.

    d. Each type of tropical fish has its own ideal water temperature.

Questions 13 – 14 refer to the following passage.

Vice President Johnson, Mr. Speaker, Mr. Chief Justice, President Eisenhower, Vice President Nixon, President Truman, reverend clergy, fellow citizens:

We observe today not a victory of party, but a celebration of freedom -- symbolizing an end, as well as a beginning -- signifying renewal, as well as change. For I have sworn before you and Almighty God the same solemn oath our forebears prescribed nearly a century and three-quarters ago.

The world is very different now. For man holds in his mortal hands the power to abolish all forms of human poverty and all forms of human life. And yet the same revolutionary beliefs for which our forebears fought are still at issue around the globe -- the belief that the rights of man come not from the generosity of the state, but from the hand of God.

We dare not forget today that we are the heirs of that first revolution. Let the word go forth from this time and place, to friend and foe alike, that the torch has been passed to a new generation of Americans -- born in this century, tempered by war, disciplined by a hard and bitter peace, proud of our ancient heritage, and unwilling to witness or permit the slow undoing of those human rights to which this nation has always been committed, and to which we are committed today at home and around the world.

Let every nation know, whether it wishes us well or ill, that we shall pay any price, bear any burden, meet any hardship, support any friend, oppose any foe, to assure the survival and the success of liberty.

This much we pledge -- and more.

John F. Kennedy Inaugural Address 20 January 1961

13. What is the tone of this speech?

    a. Triumphant

    b. Optimistic

    c. Threatening

    d. Gloating

14. Which of the following is an opinion?

a. The world is very different now.

b. For man holds in his mortal hands the power to abolish all forms of human poverty and all forms of human life.

c. We dare not forget today that we are the heirs of that first revolution

d. For I have sworn before you and Almighty God the same solemn oath our forebears prescribed nearly a century and three-quarters ago.

Reading Self-Assessment Answer Key

1. A
The passage does not mention the flu specifically, however we know the flu is a pathogen (a bacterium, virus, or other microorganism that can cause disease). Therefore, we can infer, when a person's body fights off the flu, this is the immune system in action.

2. B
The immune system's primary function is to protect against disease.

3. A
The passage refers to evolution of the immune system being important for efficiency. In paragraph three, there is a discussion of adaptive and acquired immunity, where the immune system "remembers" pathogens.

We can conclude, evolution of the immune system is an important factor in the immune system's efficiency.

4. B
The sentence that expresses the main idea of the passage is, "An immune system is a system of biological structures and processes that protects against disease by identifying and killing pathogens and other threats."

5. C
We can infer white blood cells are essential to fight off infectious diseases, from the passage, "cells of the immune system that defend the body against both infectious disease and foreign material."

6. A
We can say the number of white blood cells in a liter of blood make up about 1% of a healthy adult's blood. This is a fact-based question that is easy and fast to answer. The question asks about a percentage. You can quickly and easily scan the passage for the percent sign, or the word percent and find the answer.

7. C

A more scientific term for "white blood cell" is leukocyte, from the first paragraph, first sentence of the passage.

8. A

The white blood cell count can indicate disease (cancer). We know this from the last sentence of paragraph two, "The physical properties of white blood cells, such as volume, conductivity, and granularity, changes due to the presence of immature cells, or malignant cells."

9. B

The general tone is informal.

10. B

The statement, " Fewer people have aquariums in their office than at home," cannot be inferred from this article.

11. C

The author does not provide evidence for this statement.

12. B

The following statement is an opinion, " Aquarium gravel improves the aesthetics of the aquarium."

13. A

This is a triumphant speech where President Kennedy is celebrating his victory.

14. C

The statement, "We dare not forget today that we are the heirs of that first revolution" is an opinion.

Help with Reading Comprehension

At first sight, reading comprehension tests look challenging especially if you are given long essays to answer only two to three questions. While reading, you might notice your attention wandering, or you may feel sleepy. Do not be discouraged because there are various tactics and long range strategies that make comprehending even long, boring essays easier.

Your friends before your foes. It is always best to tackle essays or passages with familiar subjects rather than those with unfamiliar ones. This approach applies the same logic as tackling easy questions before hard ones. Skip passages that do not interest you and leave them for later when there is more time left.

Don't use 'special' reading techniques. This is not the time for speed-reading or anything like that – just plain ordinary reading – not too slow and not too fast.

Read through the entire passage and the questions before you do anything. Many students try reading the questions first and then looking for answers in the passage thinking this approach is more efficient. What these students do not realize is that it is often hard to navigate in unfamiliar roads. If you do not familiarize yourself with the passage first, looking for answers become not only time-consuming but also dangerous because you might miss the context of the answer you are looking for. If you read the questions first you will only confuse yourself and lose valuable time.

Familiarize yourself with reading comprehension questions. If you are familiar with the common types of reading questions, you are able to take note of important parts of the passage, saving time. There are six major kinds of reading questions.

- **Main Idea**- Questions that ask for the central thought or significance of the passage.

- **Specific Details** - Questions that asks for explicitly stated ideas.

- **Drawing Inferences** - Questions that ask for a statement's intended meaning.

- **Tone or Attitude** - Questions that test your ability to sense the emotional state of the author.

- **Context Meaning** – Questions that ask for the meaning of a word depending on the context.

- **Technique** – Questions that ask for the method of organization or the writing style of the author.

Read. Read. Read. The best preparation for reading comprehension tests is always to read, read and read. If you are not used to reading lengthy passages, you will probably lose concentration. Increase your attention span by making a habit out of reading.

Reading Comprehension tests become less daunting when you have trained yourself to read and understand fast. Always remember that it is easier to understand passages you are interested in. Do not read through passages hastily. Make mental notes of ideas that you think might be asked.

Reading Strategy

When facing the reading comprehension section of a standardized test, you need a strategy to be successful. You want to keep several steps in mind:

- **First, make a note of the time and the number of sections**. Time your work accordingly. Typically, four to five minutes per section is sufficient. Second, read the directions for each selection thoroughly before beginning (and listen well to any additional verbal instructions, as they will often clarify obscure or confusing written guidelines). You must know exactly how to do what you're about to do!

- **Now you're ready to begin reading the selection.** Read the passage carefully, noting significant characters or events on a scratch sheet of paper or underlining on the test sheet. Many students find making a basic list in the margins helpful. Quickly jot down or underline one-word summaries of characters, notable happenings, numbers, or key ideas. This will help you better retain information and focus wandering thoughts. Remember, however, that your main goal in doing this is to find the information that answers the questions. Even if you find the passage interesting, remember your goal and work fast but stay on track.

- Now read the question and all of the choices. Now you have read the passage, have a general idea of the main ideas, and have marked the important points. Read the question and all of the choices. Never choose an answer without reading them all! Questions are often designed to confuse – stay focussed and clear. Usually the answer choices will focus on one or two facts or inferences from the passage. Keep these clear in your mind.

- **Search for the answer.** With a very general idea of what the different choices are, go back to the passage and scan for the relevant information. Watch for big words, unusual or unique words. These make your job easier as you can scan the text for the particular word.

- Mark the Answer. Now you have the key information the question is looking for. Go back to the question, quickly scan the choices and mark the correct one.

Understand and practice the different types of standardized reading comprehension tests. See the list above for the different types. Typically, there will be several questions dealing with facts from the selection, a couple more inference questions dealing with logical consequences of those facts, and periodically an application-oriented question surfaces to force you to make connections with what you already know. Some students prefer to answer the questions as listed, and feel classifying the question and then ordering is wasting precious time. Other students prefer to answer the different types of questions in order of how easy or difficult they are. The choice is yours and do whatever works for you. If you want to try answering in order of difficulty, here is a recommended order, answer fact questions first; they're easily found within the passage. Tackle inference problems next, after re-reading the question(s) as many times as you need to. Application or 'best guess' questions usually take the longest, so save them for last.

Use the practice tests to try out both ways of answering and see what works for you.

For more help with reading comprehension, see Multiple Choice Secrets.

Main Idea and Supporting Details

Identifying the main idea, topic and supporting details in a passage can feel like an overwhelming task. The passages used for standardized tests can be boring and seem difficult - Test writers don't use interesting passages or ones that talk about things most people are familiar with. Despite these obstacles, all passages and paragraphs will have the information you need to answer the questions.

The topic of a passage or paragraph is its subject. It's the general idea and can be summed up in a word or short phrase. On some standardized tests, there is a short description of the passage if it's taken from a longer work. Make sure you read the description as it might state the topic of the passage. If not, read the passage and ask yourself, "Who or what is this about?" For example:

Over the years, school uniforms have been hotly debated. Arguments are made that students have the right to show individuality and express themselves by choosing their own clothes. However, this brings up social and academic issues. Some kids cannot afford to wear the clothes they like and might be bullied by the "better dressed" students. With attention drawn to clothes and the individual, students will lose focus on class work and the reason they are in school. School uniforms should be mandatory.

Ask: What is this paragraph about?

Topic: school uniforms

Once you have the topic, it's easier to find the main idea. The main idea is a specific statement telling what the writer wants you to know about the topic. Writers usually state the main idea as a thesis statement. If you're looking for the main idea of a single paragraph, the main idea is called the topic sentence and will probably be the first or last sentence. If you're looking for the main idea of an entire passage, look for the thesis statement in either the first or last paragraph. The main idea is usually restated in the conclusion. To find the main idea of a passage or paragraph, follow these steps:

1. Find the topic.

2. Ask yourself, "What point is the author trying to make about the topic?"

3. Create your own sentence summarizing the author's point.

4. Look in the text for the sentence closest in meaning to yours.

Look at the example paragraph again. It's already established that the topic of the paragraph is school uniforms. What is the main idea/topic sentence?

Ask: "What point is the author trying to make about school uniforms?"

Summary: Students should wear school uniforms.

Topic sentence: School uniforms should be mandatory.

Main Idea: School uniforms should be mandatory.

Each paragraph offers supporting details to explain the main idea. The details could be facts or reasons, but they will always answer a question about the main idea. What? Where? Why? When? How? How much/many? Look at the example paragraph again. You'll notice that more than one sentence answers a question about the main idea. These are the supporting details.

Main Idea: School uniforms should be mandatory.

Ask: Why? Some kids cannot afford to wear clothes they like and could be bullied by the "better dressed" kids. Supporting Detail

With attention drawn to clothes and the individual, Students will lose focus on class work and the reason they are in school. Supporting Detail

What if the author doesn't state the main idea in a topic sentence? The passage will have an implied main idea. It's not as difficult to find as it might seem. Paragraphs are always organized around ideas. To find an implied main idea, you need to know the topic and then find the relationship between the supporting details. Ask yourself, "What is the point the author is making about the relationship between the details?."

> Cocoa is what makes chocolate good for you. Chocolate comes in many varieties. These delectable flavors include milk chocolate, dark chocolate, semi-sweet, and white chocolate.

Ask: What is this paragraph about?

Topic: Chocolate

Ask: What? Where? Why? When? How? How much/many?

Supporting details: Chocolate is good for you because it is made of cocoa, Chocolate is delicious, Chocolate comes in different delicious flavors

Ask: What is the relationship between the details and what is the author's point?

Main Idea: Chocolate is good because it is healthy and it tastes good.

Testing Tips for Main Idea Questions

1. Skim the questions – not the answer choices - before reading the passage.

2. Questions about main idea might use the words "theme," "generalization," or "purpose."

3. Save questions about the main idea for last. On standardized tests like the SAT, the answers to the rest of the questions can be found in order in the passage.

3. Underline topic sentences in the passage. Most tests allow you to write in your testing booklet.

4. Answer the question in your own words before looking at the answer choices. Then match your answer with an answer choice.

5. Cross out incorrect answer choices immediately to prevent confusion.

6. If two of the answer choices mean the same thing but use different words, they are BOTH incorrect.

7. If a question asks about the whole passage, cross out the answer choices that apply only to part of it.

8. If only part of the information is correct, that answer choice is incorrect.

9. An answer choice that is too broad is incorrect. All information needs to be backed up by the passage.

10. Answer choices with extreme wording are usually incorrect.

Drawing Inferences And Conclusions

Drawing inferences and making conclusions happens all the time. In fact, you probably do it every time you read—sometimes without even realizing it! For example, remember the first time you saw the movie "The Lion King." When you meet Scar for the first time, he is trapping a helpless mouse with his sharp claws preparing to eat it. When you see this action you guess that Scar is going to be a bad character in the movie. Nothing appeared to tell you this. No caption came across the bottom of the screen that said "Bad Guy." No red arrow pointed to Scar and said "Evil Lion." No, you made an inference about his character based on the context clue you were given. You do the same thing when you read!

When you draw an inference or make a conclusion you are doing the same thing, you are making an educated guess based on the hints the author gives you. We call these hints "context clues." Scar trapping the innocent mouse is the context clue about Scar's character.

Usually you are making inferences and drawing conclusions the entire time that you are reading. Whether you realize it or not, you are constantly making educated guesses based on context clues. Think about a time you were reading a book and something happened that you were expecting to happen. You're not psychic! Actually, you were picking up on the context clues and making inferences about what was going to happen next!

Let's try an easy example. Read the following sentences and answer the questions at the end of the passage.

Shelly really likes to help people. She loves her job because she gets to help people every single day. However, Shelly has to work long hours and she can get called in the middle of the night for emergencies. She wears a white lab coat at work and usually she carries a stethoscope.

What is most likely Shelly's job?

    a. Musician
    b. Lawyer
    c. Doctor
    d. Teacher

This probably seemed easy. Drawing inferences isn't always this simple, but it is the same basic principle. How did you know Shelly was a doctor? She helps people, she works long hours, she wears a white lab coat, and she gets called in for emergencies at night. Context Clues! Nowhere in the paragraph did it say Shelly was a doctor, but you were able to draw that conclusion based on the information provided in the paragraph. This is how it's done!

There is a catch, though. Remember that when you draw inferences based on reading, you should only use the information given to you by the author. Sometimes it is easy for us to make conclusions based on knowledge that is already in our mind—but that can lead you to drawing an incorrect inference. For example, let's pretend there is a bully at your school named Brent. Now let's say you read a story and the main character's name is Brent. You could NOT infer that the character in the story is a bully just because his name is Brent. You should only use the information given to you by the author to avoid drawing the wrong conclusion.

Let's try another example. Read the passage below and answer the question.

Social media is an extremely popular new form of connecting and communicating over the internet. Since Facebook's original launch in 2004, millions of people have joined in the social media craze. In fact, it is estimated that almost 75% of all internet users aged 18 and older use some form of social media. Facebook started at Harvard University as a way to get students connected. However, it quickly grew into a worldwide phenomenon and today, the founder of Facebook, Mark Zuckerberg has an estimated net worth of 28.5 billion dollars.

Facebook is not the only social media platform, though. Other sites such as Twitter, Instagram, and Snapchat have since been invented and are quickly becoming just as popular! Many social media users actually use more than one type of social media. Furthermore, most social media sites have created mobile apps that allow people to connect via social media virtually anywhere in the world!

What is the most likely reason that other social media sites like Twitter and Instagram were created?

    a. Professors at Harvard University made it a class project.

    b. Facebook was extremely popular and other people thought they could also be successful by designing social media sites.

    c. Facebook was not connecting enough people.

    d. Mark Zuckerberg paid people to invent new social media sites because he wanted lots of competition.

Here, the correct answer is B. Facebook was extremely popular and other people thought they could also be successful by designing social media sites. How do we know this? What are the context clues? Take a look at the first paragraph. What do we know based on this paragraph? Well, one sentence refers to Facebook's original launch. This suggests that Facebook was one of the first social media sites. In addition, we know that the founder of Facebook has been extremely successful and is worth billions of dollars. From this we can infer that other people wanted to imitate Facebook's idea and become just as successful as Mark Zuckerberg.

Let's go through the other answers. If you chose A, it might be because Facebook started at Harvard University, so you drew the conclusion that all other social media sites were also started at Harvard University. However, there is no mention of class projects, professors, or students designing social media. So there doesn't seem to be enough support for choice A.

If you chose C, you might have been drawing your own conclusions based on outside information. Maybe none of your friends are on Facebook, so you made an inference that Facebook didn't connect enough people, so more sites were invented. Or maybe you think the people who connect on Facebook are too old, so you don't think Facebook connects enough people your age. This might be true, but remember inferences should be drawn from the information the author gives you!

If you chose D, you might be using the information that Mark Zuckerberg is worth over 28 billion dollars. It would be easy for him to pay others to design new sites, but remember, you need to use context clues! He is very wealthy, but that statement was giving you information about how successful Facebook was—not suggesting that he paid others to design more sites!

So remember, drawing inferences and conclusions is simply about using the information you are given to make an educated guess. You do this every single day so don't let this concept scare you. Look for the context clues, make sure they support your claim, and you'll be able to make accurate inferences and conclusions!

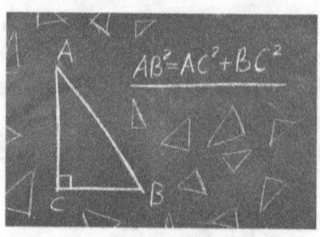

Mathematics

THIS SECTION CONTAINS A SELF-ASSESSMENT AND MATH TUTORIALS. The tutorials are designed to familiarize general principles and the self-assessment contains general questions similar to the math questions likely to be on the CAHSEE exam, but are not intended to be identical to the exam questions. The tutorials are not designed to be a complete math course, and it is assumed that students have some familiarity with math. If you do not understand parts of the tutorial, or find the tutorial difficult, it is recommended that you seek out additional instruction.

Tour of the CAHSEE Mathematics Content

The CAHSEE mathematics section has 50 questions. Below is a detailed list of the mathematics topics likely to appear on the CAHSEE. Make sure that you understand these topics at the very minimum.

- Convert decimals, percent, roman numerals and fractions

- Solve word problems

- Calculate percent and ratio

- Operations using fractions, percent and fractions

- Analyze and interpret tables, graphs and charts

- Data and Statistics

- Geometry and measurement

- Understand and solve simple algebra problems

The questions in the self-assessment are not the same as you will find on the CAHSEE - that would be too easy! And nobody knows what the questions will be and they change all the time. Mostly, the changes consist of substituting new questions for old, but the changes also can be new question formats or styles, changes to the number of questions in each section, changes to the time limits for each section, and combining sections. So, while the format and exact wording of the questions may differ slightly, and changes from year to year, if you can answer the questions below, you will have no problem with the Math section of the CAHSEE.

Mathematics Self-Assessment

The purpose of the self-assessment is:
- Identify your strengths and weaknesses.
- Develop your personalized study plan (above)
- Get accustomed to the CAHSEE format
- Extra practice – the self-assessments are almost a full 3rd practice test!

- Provide a baseline score for preparing your study schedule.

Since this is a Self-assessment, and depending on how confident you are with Math, timing yourself is optional. The CAHSEE has 50 questions, to be answered in 60 minutes. This self-assessment has 50 questions, so allow about 60 minutes to complete.

Once complete, use the table below to assess your understanding of the content, and prepare your study schedule described in chapter 1.

80% - 100%	Excellent – you have mastered the content
60 – 79%	Good. You have a working knowledge. Even though you can just pass this section, you may want to review the tutorials and do some extra practice to see if you can improve your mark.
40% - 59%	Below Average. You do not understand the content. Review the tutorials, and retake this quiz again in a few days, before proceeding to the Practice Test Questions.
Less than 40%	Poor. You have a very limited understanding. Please review the tutorials, and retake this quiz again in a few days, before proceeding to the Practice Test Questions.

Math Self-Assessment Answer Sheet

1. Ⓐ Ⓑ Ⓒ Ⓓ
2. Ⓐ Ⓑ Ⓒ Ⓓ
3. Ⓐ Ⓑ Ⓒ Ⓓ
4. Ⓐ Ⓑ Ⓒ Ⓓ
5. Ⓐ Ⓑ Ⓒ Ⓓ
6. Ⓐ Ⓑ Ⓒ Ⓓ
7. Ⓐ Ⓑ Ⓒ Ⓓ
8. Ⓐ Ⓑ Ⓒ Ⓓ
9. Ⓐ Ⓑ Ⓒ Ⓓ
10. Ⓐ Ⓑ Ⓒ Ⓓ
11. Ⓐ Ⓑ Ⓒ Ⓓ
12. Ⓐ Ⓑ Ⓒ Ⓓ
13. Ⓐ Ⓑ Ⓒ Ⓓ
14. Ⓐ Ⓑ Ⓒ Ⓓ
15. Ⓐ Ⓑ Ⓒ Ⓓ
16. Ⓐ Ⓑ Ⓒ Ⓓ
17. Ⓐ Ⓑ Ⓒ Ⓓ
18. Ⓐ Ⓑ Ⓒ Ⓓ
19. Ⓐ Ⓑ Ⓒ Ⓓ
20. Ⓐ Ⓑ Ⓒ Ⓓ
21. Ⓐ Ⓑ Ⓒ Ⓓ
22. Ⓐ Ⓑ Ⓒ Ⓓ
23. Ⓐ Ⓑ Ⓒ Ⓓ
24. Ⓐ Ⓑ Ⓒ Ⓓ
25. Ⓐ Ⓑ Ⓒ Ⓓ
26. Ⓐ Ⓑ Ⓒ Ⓓ
27. Ⓐ Ⓑ Ⓒ Ⓓ
28. Ⓐ Ⓑ Ⓒ Ⓓ
29. Ⓐ Ⓑ Ⓒ Ⓓ
30. Ⓐ Ⓑ Ⓒ Ⓓ
31. Ⓐ Ⓑ Ⓒ Ⓓ
32. Ⓐ Ⓑ Ⓒ Ⓓ
33. Ⓐ Ⓑ Ⓒ Ⓓ
34. Ⓐ Ⓑ Ⓒ Ⓓ
35. Ⓐ Ⓑ Ⓒ Ⓓ
36. Ⓐ Ⓑ Ⓒ Ⓓ
37. Ⓐ Ⓑ Ⓒ Ⓓ
38. Ⓐ Ⓑ Ⓒ Ⓓ
39. Ⓐ Ⓑ Ⓒ Ⓓ
40. Ⓐ Ⓑ Ⓒ Ⓓ
41. Ⓐ Ⓑ Ⓒ Ⓓ
42. Ⓐ Ⓑ Ⓒ Ⓓ
43. Ⓐ Ⓑ Ⓒ Ⓓ
44. Ⓐ Ⓑ Ⓒ Ⓓ
45. Ⓐ Ⓑ Ⓒ Ⓓ
46. Ⓐ Ⓑ Ⓒ Ⓓ
47. Ⓐ Ⓑ Ⓒ Ⓓ
48. Ⓐ Ⓑ Ⓒ Ⓓ
49. Ⓐ Ⓑ Ⓒ Ⓓ
50. Ⓐ Ⓑ Ⓒ Ⓓ

Mathematics Self-Assessment

Decimals, Fractions and Percent

1. A person earns $25000 per month and pays $9000 income tax per year. The Government increased income tax by 0.5% per month and his monthly earning was raised $11000. How much more income tax does he pay per month?

   a. $1260
   b. $1050
   c. $750
   d. $510

2. A boy has 5 red balls, 3 white balls and 2 yellow balls. What percent of the balls are yellow?

   a. 2%
   b. 8%
   c. 20%
   d. 12%

3. There were some oranges in a basket, by adding 8/5 of these the total became 130. How many oranges were in the basket?

   a. 60
   b. 50
   c. 40
   d. 35

4. Solve 11 + 19 x 2

    a. 60
    b. 50
    c. 49
    d. 54

5. A 7 centimeter diameter pizza weighs 750 grams. If the diameter increased to 8.2 centimeters, how much more will it weigh?

    a. 279
    b. 129
    c. 185
    d. 305

6. Solve 7 + 2 x (6 + 3) ÷ 3 - 7

    a. 20
    b. 15
    c. 7
    d. 4

7. A distributor purchased 550 kilogram potatoes for $165. He distributed all these at a rate of $6.4 per 20 kilograms to 15 shops, $3.4 per 10 kilograms to 12 shops and remaining at $1.8. If his distribution cost is $10 then what will be his profit?

    a. $10.40
    b. $8.60
    c. $14.90
    d. $23.40

8. **Convert 0.45 to a fraction**

   a. 7/20
   b. 7/45
   c. 9/20
   d. 3/20

9. **How much pay does Mr. Johnson receive if he gives half of his pay to his family, $250 to his landlord, and has exactly 3/7 of his pay left after these expenses?**

   a. $3600
   b. $3500
   c. $2800
   d. $1750

10. **What is the square root of $\sqrt{225}$?**

    a. 25
    b. 15
    c. 5
    d. 13

11. **A man buys an item for $420 and has a balance of 3000.00. How much did he have before?**

    a. $2,580
    b. $3,420
    c. $2,420
    d. $342

12. **Divide 9.60 by 3.2**

    a. 2.50
    b. 3
    c. 2.3
    d. 6.4

Mathematics

13. If a discount of 20% is given for a desk and Mark saves $45, how much did he pay for the desk?

   a. $225
   b. $160
   c. $180
   d. $210

14. 10% of p is also 1/5 of q. Which of the following is correct?

   a. p + p = q
   b. q/p = p
   c. p - q = q
   d. p/q = p

Basic Algebra

15. If X = 7 solve 3x + 5 − 2x

   a. x = 6
   b. x = 12
   c. x = 1
   d. x = 0

16. Solve the following equation 3(2x − 2) = 24 − 3x

   a. x = 24
   b. x = 9
   c. x = 10
   d. x = 2

17. Expand (x+7) (x-3)

a. $x^2 + 4x - 21$
b. $x + 21$
c. $2x + 4 - 21$
d. $6x - 21\ 2x + 4x - 21$

18. Find the solution to this inequality x + 3 > 12

a. $x < 9$
b. $x > 9$
c. $x = 9$
d. $x = 10$

19. Find the mean of 100, 1050, 320, 600 and 150.

a. 333
b. 444
c. 440
d. 320

20. The following numbers represent the ages of people on a bus – 3, 6, 27, 13, 6, 8, 12, 20, 5, 10. Calculate the mean of their ages.

a. 11
b. 6
c. 9
d. 110

Exponents

21. Express in 3^4 standard form

    a. 81
    b. 27
    c. 12
    d. 9

22. Simplify $4^3 + 2^4$

    a. 45
    b. 108
    c. 80
    d. 48

23. If $x = 2$ and $y = 5$, solve $xy^3 - x^3$

    a. 240
    b. 258
    c. 248
    d. 242

24. $X^3 \times X^2 =$

    a. 5^x
    b. x^{-5}
    c. x^{-1}
    d. X^5

25. Express 100000^0 in standard form.

    a. 1
    b. 0
    c. 100000
    d. 1000

26. Solve $\sqrt{144}$

    a. 14
    b. 72
    c. 24
    d. 12

27. Convert 7,892,000,000 to scientific notation

    a. 7.892×10^{10}
    b. 7.892×10^{-9}
    c. 7.892×10^{9}
    d. 0.7892×10^{11}

28. Convert 2.63×10^{-2}

    a. 0.00263
    b. 0.0263
    c. 0.263
    d. 2.63

Geometry

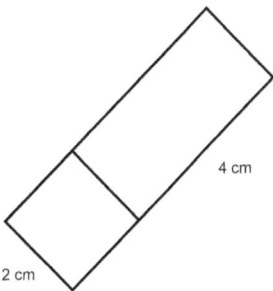

Note: figure not drawn to scale

29. Assuming the shape with 2cm side is square, what is the perimeter of the above shape?

   a. 12 cm
   b. 16 cm
   c. 6 cm
   d. 20 cm

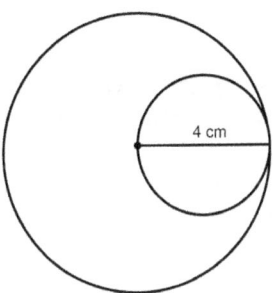

Note: figure not drawn to scale

30. Assuming the diameter of the small circle is the radius of the large circle, what is (area of large circle) - (area of small circle) in the figure above?

a. 8 π cm²
b. 10 π cm²
c. 12 π cm²
d. 16 π cm²

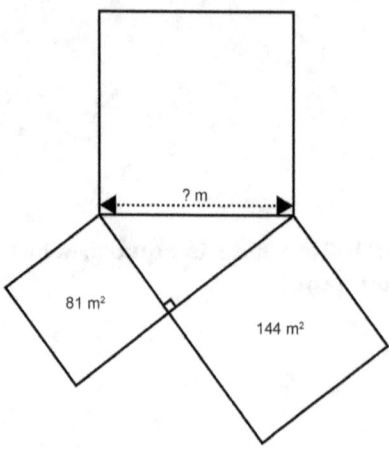

Note: figure not drawn to scale

31. Assuming the shapes around the right triangle are square, what is the length of each side of the indicated square above?

a. 10
b. 15
c. 20
d. 5

32. Order the shapes above from 1-4.

    a. Parallelogram, rectangle, trapezium, kite
    b. Rectangle, parallelogram, trapezium, kite
    c. Trapezium, rectangle, parallelogram, kite
    d. Kite, rectangle, parallelogram, trapezium

33. A bag contains 38 black balls and 42 white balls. What is the ratio of black balls to white?

    a. 9:11
    b. 1:3
    c. 19:21
    d. 11:9

34. The ratio of 8:5 = (?)%

    a. 75%
    b. 150%
    c. 175%
    d. 160%

35. 3 boys are asked to clean a surface that is 4 ft². If the portion is divided equally among the boys, what size will each of them clean?

    a. 1 ft 6 inches²
    b. 14 inches²
    c. 1 ft 2 inches²
    d. 1 ft² 48 in²

36. Brian jogged 7 times around a circular track 75 meters in diameter. How much linear distance did he cover?

    a. 1250 meters
    b. 1650 meters
    c. 1450 meters
    d. 1725 meters

37. Consider the following population growth chart.

Country	Population 2000	Population 2005
Japan	122,251,000	128,057,000
China	1,145,195,000	1,341,335,000
United States	253,339,000	310,384,000
Indonesia	184,346,000	239,871,000

Which country is growing the fastest?

    a. Japan
    b. China
    c. United States
    d. Indonesia

Linear Equations

38. Solve the linear equation: -x - 7 = -3x - 9

    a. -1
    b. 0
    c. 1
    d. 2

39. Solve the system
4x - y = 5
x + 2y = 8

    a. (3,2)
    b. (3,3)
    c. (2,3)
    d. (2,2)

Congruence

40. Consider 2 triangles ABC and A'B'C'

    AB = A' B'
    RA = RA'
    RB = RB'

Are these 2 triangles congruent?

    a. Yes
    b. No
    c. Not enough information

Basic Math

41. 389 + 454 =

    a. 853
    b. 833
    c. 843
    d. 863

42. 8,390 - 5,239 =

    a. 3,261
    b. 3,151
    c. 3,161
    d. 3,101

43. 149 × 7 =

    a. 1032
    b. 1043
    c. 1059
    d. 1063

44. 467 × 41 =

    a. 19,147
    b. 21,227
    c. 23,107
    d. 18,177

45. 1518 ÷ 27 =

    a. 54 r1
    b. 56 r6
    c. 55 r3
    d. 59 r2

46. 7050 − 305 =

    a. 6705
    b. 6745
    c. 5745
    d. 6045

47. 8327 − 1278 =

    a. 7149
    b. 7209
    c. 6059
    d. 7049

48. 285 × 12 =

    a. 3420
    b. 3402
    c. 3024
    d. 2322

49. 46 × 15 =

    a. 590
    b. 690
    c. 490
    d. 790

50. 5575 + 8791 =

    a. 14,756
    b. 14,566
    c. 14,466
    d. 14,366

Answer Key

Decimals, Percent and Fractions

1. D
The income tax per year is $9,000. So, the income tax per month is 9,000/12 = $750.

This person earns $25,000 per month and pays $750 income tax. We need to find the rate of the income tax:

Tax rate: 750•100/25,000 = 3%

Government increased this rate by 0.5% so it became 3.5%.

The income of the person per month is increased $11,000 so it became: $25,000 + $11,000 = $36,000.

The new monthly income tax is: 36,000•3.5/100 = $1260.

Amount of increase in tax per month is: $1260 - $750 = $510.

2. C
Total no. of balls = 10, no. of yellow balls = 2, answer = 2/10 X 100 = 20%

3. B
Suppose oranges in the basket before = x, Then: X + 8x/5 = 130, 5x + 8x = 650, so X = 50.

4. C
Do multiplication first - 19 X 2 = 38, then addition, 38 + 11 = 49.

5. A
The area of a 7 centimeter pizza is $\prod(3.5)^2$ × = 38.48 cm². The weight of 1 cm² of pizza will be 750/38.48 = 19.49 grams. The area of 8.2 centimeter diameter pizza is $\prod (4.1)^2$ = 52.81 cm². The difference in area is 52.81 – 38.48 = 14.33 cm². The difference in weight will be 19.49 X 14.33 = 279.29 grams.

6. A

7 + 2 x (6 + 3) ÷ 3 - 7 = 6. Order of operations - do brackets first, then multiplication and division.

7 + 2 X (9) ÷ 3 - 7
9 X 9 ÷ 3 - 7
81 ÷ 3 - 7
27 - 7 = 20

7. B

The distribution is done in three different rates and amounts:

$6.4 per 20 kilograms to 15 shops ... 20•15 = 300 kilograms distributed

$3.4 per 10 kilograms to 12 shops ... 10•12 = 120 kilograms distributed

550 - (300 + 120) = 550 - 420 = 130 kilograms left. This amount is distributed by 5 kilogram portions. So, this means that there are 130/5 = 26 shops.

$1.8 per 130 kilograms.

We need to find the amount he earned overall these distributions.

$6.4 per 20 kilograms : 6.4•15 = $96 for 300 kilograms

$3.4 per 10 kilograms : 3.4•12 = $40.8 for 120 kilograms

$1.8 per 5 kilograms : 1.8•26 = $46.8 for 130 kilograms

So, he earned 96 + 40.8 + 46.8 = $ 183.6

The total distribution cost is given as $10

The profit is found by: Money earned - money spent ... It is important to remember that he bought 550 kilograms of potatoes for $165 at the beginning:

Profit = 183.6 - 10 - 165 = $8.6

8. C
0.45 = 45/100 = 9/20

9. B
We check the fractions in the question and see that there is a "half" (that is 1/2) and 3/7. So, we multiply the denominators of these fractions to decide how to name the total money. We say that Mr. Johnson has 14x at the beginning; he gives half of this, meaning 7x, to his family. $250 to his landlord. He has 3/7 of his money left. 3/7 of 14x is equal to:

14x•(3/7) = 6x

So,

Spent money is: 7x + 250

Unspent money is: 6x

Total money is: 14x

We write an equation: total money = spent money + unspent money

14x = 7x + 250 + 6x

14x - 7x - 6x = 250

x = 250

We are asked to find the total money that is 14x:

14x = 14•250 = $3500

10. B
√225 = 15.

11. B
(Amount Spent) $420 + $3000 (Balance) = $3420

12. B
9.60/3.2 = 3

13. C
By the given information in the question, we understand that the discounted part is the saved amount. If we say that the original price of the desk is 100x; by 20% discount rate, 20x will be the discounted part:

20x = 45

We know that Mark paid 20% less than the original price. So, he paid 100x - 20x = 80x. We are asked to find 80x. With a simple direct proportion, we can find the result:

20x = 45

80x = ?

By cross multiplication, we find the result:

? = 80x•45 / 20x = 4•45 = $180

14. C
First convert to percent. 1/5 = 20%, so 10% of p = 20% of q, and p = 2 X q, and p - q = q

15. B
X=7, so 3x = 3 x 7 = 21, 2x = 2 x 7 = 14, so 21 + 5 - 14 = 26 - 14 = 12

16. D
6x – 6 = 24 – 3x, = 6x + 3x -6 = 24, = 9x – 6 = 24, = 9x = 24 – 6, = 9x = 18, = x = 18/9, = x = 2

17. A
Multiply the first bracket and the second. x^2 - 3x + 7x - 21 = x^2 + 4x – 21

18. B
X > 12 – 3, = x > 9

19. B
First add all the numbers 100 + 1050 + 320 + 600 + 150 = 2220. Then divide by 5 (the number of data provided) = 2220/5 = 444

20. A
First add all the numbers 3 + 6 + 27 + 13 + 6 + 8 + 12 + 20 + 5 + 10 = 110. Then divide by 10 (the number of data provided) = 110/10 = 11.

Exponents

21. A
3 x 3 x 3 x 3 = 81

22. C
(4 x 4 x 4) + (2 x 2 x 2 x 2) = 64 + 16 = 80

23. D
$2(5)^3 - (2)^3 = 2(125) - 8 = 250 - 8 = 242$

24. D
$X^3 \times X^2 = X^{3+2} = X^5$
To multiply exponents with like bases, add the exponents.

25. A
Any value (except 0) raised to the power of 0 equals 1.

26. D
$\sqrt{144} = 12$

27. C
The decimal point moves 9 spaces right to be placed after 7, which is the first non-zero number. Thus 7.892 x 10^9

28. B
The scientific notation is in the negative so we shift the decimal 2 places to the left. Thus its 0.0263.

Geometry

29. B
We see that there is a square with side 2 cm and a rectangle adjacent to it, with one side 2 cm (common side with the square) and the other side 4 cm. The perimeter of a shape is found by summing up all sides surrounding the shape, not adding the ones inside the shape. Three 2 cm sides from

the square, and two 4 cm sides and one 2 cm side from the rectangle contribute the perimeter.

So, the perimeter of the shape is: 2 + 2 + 2 + 4 + 2 + 4 = 16 cm.

30. C
In the figure, we are given a large circle and a small circle inside it; with the diameter equal to the radius of the large one. The diameter of the small circle is 4 cm. This means that its radius is 2 cm. Since the diameter of the small circle is the radius of the large circle, the radius of the large circle is 4 cm. The area of a circle is calculated by: πr^2 where r is the radius.

Area of the small circle: $\pi(2)^2 = 4\pi$

Area of the large circle: $\pi(4)^2 = 16\pi$

The difference area is found by:

Area of the large circle - Area of the small circle = $16\pi - 4\pi = 12\pi$

31. B
We see that there are three squares forming a right triangle in the middle. Two of the squares have the areas 81 m² and 144 m². If we denote their sides a and b respectively:

$a^2 = 81$ and $b^2 = 144$. The length which is asked is the hypotenuse; a and b are the opposite and adjacent sides of the right angle. By using the Pythagorean Theorem, we can find the value of the asked side:

Pythagorean Theorem:

(Hypotenuse)² = (Opposite Side)² + (Adjacent Side)²

$h^2 = a^2 + b^2$

$a^2 = 81$ and $b^2 = 144$ are given. So;

$h^2 = 81 + 144$

$h^2 = 225$

$h = 15$ m

32. B
Rectangle, parallelogram, trapezium, kite

33. C
The ratio of black balls to white is 38:42. Reduce to lowest terms = 19:21

34. D
The ratio 8:5 = X/100
X = 160%

35. D
1 foot is equal to 12 inches. So 1 ft² = 12•12 in²
4 ft² = 4•12•12 in² = 576 in²

This amount of surface area is divided equally among 3 boys.

Each boy will clean 576/3 = 192 in²

192 in² = 144 in² + 48 in²; 144 in² = 1 ft²

So, each boy will clean 1 ft² and 48 in²

36. B
In one round trip he covers the distance equal to the circumference of the circular path. 75/X = 3.14159. 75 X 3.14159 = X. Circumference of the path = X = 235.65 meters. Distance covered 7 times around = 235.65 × 7 = 1650 meters.

37. D
Indonesia is growing the fastest at about 30%.

Linear Equations

38. A
We should collect similar terms on the same side. Here, we can collect x terms on left side, and the constants on the right side:

- x - 7 = - 3x - 9 .... Let us add 3x to both sides:

- x - 7 + 3x = - 3x - 9 + 3x

2x - 7 = - 9 ... Now, we can add + 7 to both sides:

$2x - 7 + 7 = -9 + 7$

$2x = -2$ ... Dividing both sides by 2 gives us the value of x:

$x = -2/2$

$x = -1$

39. C
First, we need to write two equations separately:
$4x - y = 5$ (I)

$x + 2y = 8$ (II) ... Here, we can use two ways to solve the system. One is substitution method, the other one is linear elimination method:

<u>1. Substitution Method</u>:

Equation (I) gives us that $y = 4x - 5$. We insert this value of y into equation (II):

$x + 2(4x - 5) = 8$

$x + 8x - 10 = 8$

$9x - 10 = 8$

$9x = 18$

$x = 2$

Bu knowing $x = 2$, we can find the value of y by inserting $x = 2$ into either of the equations. Let us choose equation (I):

$4(2) - y = 5$

$8 - y = 5$

$8 - 5 = y$

$y = 3$ → solution is (2, 3)

<u>2. Linear Elimination Method</u>:

2•/ $4x - y = 5$ ... by multiplying equation (I) by 2, we see that $-2y$ will form; and y terms

$x + 2y = 8$ ... will be eliminated when summed with $+2y$ in equation (II):

2•/ 4x - y = 5

+   x + 2y = 8

   8x - 2y = 10

+ x + 2y = 8 ... Summing side by side:

8x + x - 2y + 2y = 10 + 8 ... -2y and +2y eliminate each other:

9x = 18

x = 2

By knowing x = 2, we can find the value of y by inserting x = 2 into either of the equations. Let us choose equation (I):

4(2) - y = 5

8 - y = 5

8 - 5 = y

y = 3 → solution is (2, 3)

Congruence

40. A
The triangles are congruent. This is a case of ASA:

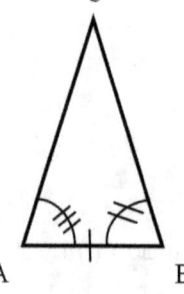 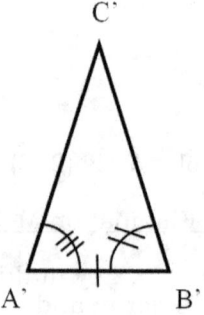

41. C
389 + 454 = 843

42. B
8,390 - 5,239 = 3,151

43. B
149 X 7 = 1043

44. A
467 × 41 = 19147

45. B
1518 ÷ 27 = 56 r6

46. B
7050 − 305 = 6745

47. D
8327 − 1278 = 7049

48. A
285 × 12 = 3420

49. B
46 × 15 = 690

50. D
5575 + 8791 = 14366

Fraction Tips, Tricks and Shortcuts

When you are writing an exam, time is precious, and anything you can do to answer questions faster, is a real advantage. Here are some ideas, shortcuts, tips and tricks that can speed up answering fraction problems.

Remember that a fraction is just a number which names a portion of something. For instance, instead of having a whole pie, a fraction says you have a part of a pie--such as a half of one or a fourth of one.

Two digits make up a fraction. The digit on top is known as the numerator. The digit on the bottom is known as the denominator. To remember which is which, just remember that "denominator" and "down" both start with a "d." And the "downstairs" number is the denominator. So for instance, in ½, the numerator is the 1 and the denominator (or "downstairs") number is the 2.

- ☐ It's easy to add two fractions if they have the same denominator. Just add the digits on top and leave the bottom one the same: 1/10 + 6/10 = 7/10.

- ☐ It's the same with subtracting fractions with the same denominator: 7/10 - 6/10 = 1/10.

- ☐ Adding and subtracting fractions with different denominators is a little more complicated. First, you have to get the problem so that they do have the same denominators. The easiest way to do this is to multiply the denominators: For 2/5 + 1/2 multiply 5 by 2. Now you have a denominator of 10. But now you have to change the top numbers too. Since you multiplied the 5 in 2/5 by 2, you also multiply the 2 by 2, to get 4. So the first number is now 4/10. Since you multiplied the second number times 5, you also multiply its top number by 5, to get a final fraction of 5/10. Now you can add 5 and 4 together to get a final sum of 9/10.

- ☐ Sometimes you'll be asked to reduce a fraction to its simplest form. This means getting it to where the only common factor of the numerator and denominator is 1. Think of it this way: Numerators and denominators are brothers that must be treated the same. If you do something to one, you must do it to the other, or it's just not fair. For instance, if you divide your numerator by 2, then you should also divide the denominator by the same. Let's take an example: The fraction 2/10 . This is not reduced to its simplest terms because there is a number that will divide evenly into both: the number 2. We want to make it so that the only number that will divide

Mathematics 69

evenly into both is 1. What can we divide into 2 to get 1? The number 2, of course! Now to be "fair," we have to do the same thing to the denominator: Divide 2 into 10 and you get 5. So our new, reduced fraction is 1/5.

- In some ways, multiplying fractions is the easiest of all: Just multiply the two top numbers and then multiply the two bottom numbers. For instance, with this problem:
2/5 X 2/3 you multiply 2 by 2 and get a top number of 4; then multiply 5 by 3 and get a bottom number of 15. Your answer is 4/15.

- Dividing fractions is a bit more involved, but still not too hard. You once again multiply, but only AFTER you have turned the second fraction upside-down. To divide ⅞ by ½, turn the ½ into 2/1, then multiply the top numbers and multiply the bottom numbers: ⅞ X 2/1 gives us 14 on top and 8 on the bottom.

Converting Fractions to Decimals

There are a couple of ways to become good at converting fractions to decimals. One -- the one that will make you the fastest in basic math skills -- is to learn some basic fraction facts. It's a good idea, if you're good at memory, to memorize the following:

1/100 is one hundredth, or .01.

1/50 is two hundredths, or .02.

1/25 is one twenty-fifths or four hundredths, or .04.

1/20 is one twentieth or five hundredths, or .05.

1/10 is one tenth, or .1.

1/8 is one eighth, or one hundred twenty-five thousandths, or .125.

1/5 is one fifth, or two tenths, or .2.

1/4 is one fourth or twenty-five hundredths, or .25.

1/3 is one third or thirty-three hundredths, or .33.

1/2 is one half or five tenths, or .5.

3/4 is three fourths, or seventy-five hundredths, or .75.

Of course, if you're no good at memorization, another good technique for converting a fraction to a decimal is to manipulate it so that the fraction's denominator is 10, 10, 1000, or some other power of 10. Here's an example: We'll start with ¾. What is the first number in the 4 "times table" that you can multiply and get a multiple of 10? Can you multiply 4 by something to get 10? No. Can you multiply it by something to get 100? Yes! 4 X 25 is 100. So let's take that 25 and multiply it by the numerator in our fraction ¾. The numerator is 3, and 3 X 25 is 75. We'll move the decimal in 75 all the way to the left, and we find that ¾ is .75.

We'll do another one: 1/5. Again, we want to find a power of 10 that 5 goes into evenly. Will 5 go into 10? Yes! It goes 2 times. So we'll take that 2 and multiply it by our numerator, 1, and we get 2. We move the decimal in 2 all the way to the left and find that 1/5 is equal to .2.

Converting Fractions to Percent

Working with either fractions or percents can be intimidating enough. But converting from one to the other? That's a genuine nightmare for those who are not math wizards. But really, it doesn't have to be that way. Here are two ways to make it easier and faster to convert a fraction to a percent.

- ☐ First, you might remember that a fraction is nothing more than a division problem: you're dividing the bottom number into the top number. So for instance, if we start with a fraction 1/10, we are making a division problem with the 10 on the outside the bracket and the 1 on the inside. As you remember from your lessons on dividing by decimals, since 10 won't go into 1, you add a decimal and make it 10 into 1.0. 10 into 10 goes 1 time, and since it's behind the decimal, it's .1. And how do we say .1? We say "one tenth," which is exactly what we started with: 1/10. So we have a number we can work with now: .1. When we're dealing with percents, though, we're dealing strictly with hundredths (not tenths). You remember from studying decimals that adding a zero to the right of the number on the right side of the decimal does not change the value. Therefore, we can change .1 into .10 and have the same number--except now it's expressed as hundredths. We have 10 hundredths. That's ten out of 100--which is just another way of saying ten percent (ten per hundred or ten out of 100). In other words .1 = .10 = 10 percent. Remember, if you're changing from a decimal to a percent, get rid of the decimal on the left and replace it with a percent mark on the right: 10%. Let's review those steps again: Divide 10 into 1. Since 10 doesn't go into 1, turn 1 into 1.0. Now divide 10 into 1.0. Since 10 goes into 10 1 time, put it there and add your decimal to make it .1. Since a percent is always "hundredths," let's change .1 into .10. Then remove the decimal on the left and replace with a percent sign on the right. The answer is 10%.

☐ If you're doing these conversions on a multiple-choice test, here's an idea that might be even easier and faster. Let's say you have a fraction of 1/8 and you're asked what the percent is. Since we know that "percent" means hundredths, ask yourself what number we can multiply 8 by to get 100. Since there is no number, ask what number gets us close to 100. That number is 12: 8 X 12 = 96. So it gets us a little less than 100. Now, whatever you do to the denominator, you have to do to the numerator. Let's multiply 1 X 12 and we get 12. However, since 96 is a little less than 100, we know that our answer will be a percent a little MORE than 12%. So if your possible answers on the multiple-choice test are these:

a) 8.5%   b) 19%   c) 12.5%   d) 25%

then we know the answer is c) 12.5%, because it's a little MORE than the 12 we got in our math problem above.

Another way to look at this, using multiple choice strategy is you know the answer will be "about" 12. Looking at the other choices, they are either too large or too small and can be eliminated right away.

This was an easy example to demonstrate, so don't be fooled! You probably won't get such an easy question on your exam, but the principle holds just the same. By estimating your answer quickly, you can eliminate choices immediately and save precious exam time.

Decimal Tips, Tricks and Shortcuts

Converting Decimals to Fractions

One of the most important tricks for correctly converting a decimal to a fraction doesn't involve math at all. It's simply to learn to say the decimal correctly. If you say "point one" or "point 25" for .1 and .25, you'll have more trouble getting the conversion correct. However, if you know that it's called "one tenth" and "twenty-five hundredths," you're on the way to a correct conversion. That's because, if you know your fractions, you know that "one tenth" looks like this: 1/10. And "twenty-five hundredths" looks like this: 25/100.

Even if you have digits before the decimal, such as 3.4, learning how to say the word will help you with the conversion into a fraction. It's not "three point four," it's "three and four tenths." Knowing this, you know that the fraction which looks like "three and four tenths" is 3 4/10.

Of course, your conversion is not complete until you reduce the fraction to its lowest terms: It's not 25/100, but 1/4.

Converting Decimals to Percent

Changing a decimal to a percent is easy if you remember one math formula: multiply by 100. For instance, if you start with .45, you change it to a percent by simply multiplying it by 100. You then wind up with 45. Add the % sign to the end and you get 45%.

That seems easy enough, right? Here think of it this way: You just take out the decimal and stick in a percent sign on the opposite sign. In other words, the decimal on the left is replaced by the % on the right.

It doesn't work that easily if the decimal is in the middle of the number. Let's use 3.7 for example. Here, take out the decimal in the middle and replace it with a 0 % at the end. So 3.7 converted to decimal is 370%.

Percent Tips, Tricks and Shortcuts

Percent problems are not nearly as scary as they appear, if you remember this neat trick:

Draw a cross as in:

Portion	Percent
Whole	100

In the upper left, write PORTION. In the bottom left write WHOLE. In the top right, write PERCENT and in the bottom right, write 100. Whatever your problem is, you will leave blank the unknown, and fill in the other four parts. For example, let's suppose your problem is: Find 10% of 50. Since we know the 10% part, we put 10 in the percent corner. Since the whole number in our problem is 50, we put that in the corner marked whole. You always put 100 underneath the percent, so we leave it as is, which leaves only the top left corner blank. This is where we'll put our answer. Now simply multiply the two corner numbers that are NOT 100. Here, it's 10 X 50. That gives us 500. Now multiply this by the remaining corner, or 100, to get a final answer of 5. 5 is the number that goes in the upper-left corner, and is your final solution.

Another hint to remember: Percents are the same thing as hundredths in decimals. So .45 is the same as 45 hundredths or 45 percent.

Converting Percents to Decimals

Percents are simply a specific type of decimals, so it should be no surprise that converting between the two is actually fairly simple. Here are a few tricks and shortcuts to keep in mind:

- Remember that percent literally means "per 100" or "for every 100." So when you speak of 30% you're saying 30 for every 100 or the fraction 30/100. In basic math, you learned that fractions that have 10 or 100 as the denominator can easily be turned into a decimal. 30/100 is thirty hundredths, or expressed as a decimal, .30.
- Another way to look at it: To convert a percent to a decimal, simply divide the number by 100. So for instance, if the percent is 47%, divide 47 by 100. The result will be .47. Get rid of the % mark and you're done.
- Remember that the easiest way of dividing by 100 is by moving your decimal two spots to the left.

Converting Percents to Fractions

Converting percents to fractions is easy. After all, a percent is nothing except a type of fraction; it tells you what part of 100 that you're talking about. Here are some simple ideas for making the conversion from a percent to a fraction:

Mathematics 75

- If the percent is a whole number -- say 34% -- then simply write a fraction with 100 as the denominator (the bottom number). Then put the percentage itself on top. So 34% becomes 34/100.
- Now reduce as you would reduce any percent. Here, by dividing 2 into 34 and 2 into 100, you get 17/50.
- If your percent is not a whole number -- say 3.4% --then convert it to a decimal expressed as hundredths. 3.4 is the same as 3.40 (or 3 and forty hundredths). Now ask yourself how you would express "three and forty hundredths" as a fraction. It would, of course, be 3 40/100. Reduce this and it becomes 3 2/5.

Exponents: Tips, Shortcuts & Tricks

Exponents seem like advanced math to most—like some mysterious code with a complicated meaning. In fact, though, an exponent is just short hand for saying that you're multiplying a number by itself two or more times. For instance, instead of saying that you're multiplying 5 x 5 x 5, you can show that you're multiplying 5 by itself 3 times if you just write 5^3. We usually say this as "five to the third power" or "five to the power of three." In this example, the raised 3 is an "exponent," while the 5 is the "base." You can even use exponents with fractions. For instance, $1/2^3$ means you're multiplying 1/2 x 1/2 x 1/2. (The answer is 1/8). Some other helpful hints for working with exponents:

- Here's how to do basic multiplication of exponents. If you have the same number with a different exponent (For instance 5^3 X 5^2) just add the exponents and multiply the bases as usual. The answer, then, is 25^5.
- This doesn't work, though, if the bases are different. For instance, in 5^3 X 3^2 we simply have to do the math the long way to figure out the final solution: 5 x 5 x 5, multiplying that result times the result for 3 X 2. (The answer is 750).
- Looking at it from the opposite side, to divide two exponents with the same base (or bottom number), subtract the smaller exponent from the larger one. If

we were dividing the problem above, we would subtract the 2 from the 3 to get 1. 5 to the power of 1 is simply 5.

• One time when thinking of exponents as merely multiplication doesn't work is when the raised number is zero. Any number raised to the "zeroth" power is 1 (Not, as we tend to think, zero).

Number (x)	x^2	x^3
1	1	1
2	4	8
3	9	27
4	16	64
5	25	125
6	36	216
7	49	343
8	64	512
9	81	729
10	100	1000
11	121	1331
12	144	1728
13	169	2197
14	196	2744
15	225	3375
16	256	4096

Mean, Median and Mode

Mean, mode and median are basic statistical tools used to calculate different types of averages.

Mean

Mean is the most common form of average used. To calculate mean, you simple add up all the values of data given and divide by the number data provided.

Example

Find the mean of 8, 5, 7, 10, 15, 21
Sum of values = 8 + 5 + 7 + 10 + 15 + 21 = 66
Number of data = 6
Mean = 66/6 = 11

Median

Median refers to the middle value among a set or series of values after they have been arranged in numerical order. Median thus means the middle of the set of values. When two numbers fall in the middle, you simple add the value of the two numbers and divide by 2 to get the middle of the two numbers.

Example

Arrange these numbers in ascending order and then find the median
First arrange in ascending order 8, 5, 7, 10, 15, 21
= 5, 7, 8, 10, 15, 21

There are 6 numbers on the series and two fall in the middle
= 8 and 10
The median = 8 + 10/2
= 18/2 = 9

Mode

Mode refers to the most occurring number or value among a set of values. Note that it is possible not to have a most occurring number and then the answer becomes 'No Mode'

Example

8, 5, 7, 10, 15, 21, 5, 7, 2, 5

Mode refers to the most occurring number
8, 10, 15, 2 and 21 occur once
5 occurs 3 times
7 occurs 2 times

The most occurring number is 5, which occurs three times.

How to Answer Basic Math Multiple Choice

Math is the one section where you need to make sure that you understand the processes before you ever tackle it. That's because the time allowed on the math portion is typically so short that there's not much room for error. You have to be fast and accurate. It's imperative that before the test day arrives, you've learned all of the main formulas that will be used, and then to create your own problems (and solve them).

On the actual test day, use the "Plug-Check-Check" strategy. Here's how it goes.

Read the problem, but not the answers. You'll want to work the problem first and come up with your own answers. If you did the work right, you should find your answer among the choices given.

If you need help with the problem, plug actual numbers into the variables given. You'll find it easier to work with numbers than it is to work with letters. For instance, if the question asks, "If Y - 4 is 2 more than Z, then Y+5 is how much more than Z?" try selecting a value for Y. Let's take 6. Your question now becomes, "If 6-4 is 2 more than Z, then 6 plus 5 is how much more than Z?" Now your answer should be easier to work with.

Check the answer choices to see if your answer matches one of those. If so, select it.

If no answer matches the one you got, re-check your math, but this time, use a different method. In math, it's common for there to be more than one way to solve a problem. As a simple example, if you multiplied 12 X 13 and did not get an answer that matches one of the answer choices, you might try adding 13 together 12 different times and see if you get a good answer.

Math Multiple Choice Strategy

The two strategies for working with basic math multiple choice are Estimation and Elimination.

Math Strategy 1 - Estimation.

Just like it sounds, try to estimate an approximate answer first. Then look at the choices.

Math Strategy 2 - Elimination.

For every question, no matter what type, eliminating obviously incorrect answers narrows the possible choices. Elimination is probably the most powerful strategy for answering multiple choice.

Here are a few basic math examples of how this works.

Solve 2/3 + 5/12

    a. 9/17
    b. 3/11
    c. 7/12
    d. 1 1/12

First estimate the answer. 2/3 is more than half and 5/12 is about half, so the answer is going to be very close to 1.

Next, Eliminate. Choice A is about 1/2 and can be eliminated, Choice B is very small, less than 1/2 and can be eliminated. Choice C is close to 1/2 and can be eliminated. Leaving only Choice D, which is just over 1.

Work through the solution, a common denominator is needed, a number which both 3 and 12 will divide into.
2/3 = 8/12. So, 8+5/12 = 13/12 = 1 1/12

Choice D is correct.

Solve 4/5 – 2/3

    a. 2/2

    b. 2/13

    c. 1

    d. 2/15

You can eliminate Choice A, because it is 1 and since both of the numbers are close to one, the difference is going to be very small. You can eliminate Choice C for the same reason.

Next, look at the denominators. Since 5 and 3 don't go in to 13, you can eliminate Choice B as well.

That leaves Choice D.

Checking the answer, the common denominator will be 15. So 12-10/15 = 2/15. Choice D is correct.

Fractions shortcut - Cancelling out.

In any operation with fractions, if the numerator of one fractions has a common multiple with the denominator of the other, you can cancel out. This saves time and simplifies the problem quickly, making it easier to manage.

Solve 2/15 ÷ 4/5

    a. 6/65

    b. 6/75

    c. 5/12

d. 1/6

To divide fractions, we multiply the first fraction with the inverse of the second fraction. Therefore we have 2/15 x 5/4. The numerator of the first fraction, 2, shares a multiple with the denominator of the second fraction, 4, which is 2. These cancel out, which gives, 1/3 x 1/2 = 1/6

Cancelling Out solved the questions very quickly, but we can still use multiple choice strategies to answer.

Choice B can be eliminated because 75 is too large a denominator. Choice C can be eliminated because 5 and 15 don't go in to 12.

Choice D is correct.

Decimal Multiple Choice strategy and Shortcuts.

Multiplying decimals gives a very quick way to estimate and eliminate choices. Anytime that you multiply decimals, it is going to give an answer with the same number of decimal places as the combined operands.

So for example,

2.38 X 1.2 will produce a number with three places of decimal, which is 2.856.

Here are a few examples with step-by-step explanation:

Solve 2.06 x 1.2

    a. 24.82

    b. 2.482

    c. 24.72

    d. 2.472

This is a simple question, but even before you start calculating, you can eliminate several choices. When multiplying decimals, there will always be as many numbers behind the decimal place in the answer as the sum of the ones in the initial problem, so Choice A and C can be eliminate.

The correct answer is D: 2.06 x 1.2 = 2.472

Solve 20.0 ÷ 2.5

   a. 12.05

   b. 9.25

   c. 8.3

   d. 8

First estimate the answer to be around 10, and eliminate Choice A. And since it'd also be an even number, you can eliminate Choice B and C., leaving only choice D.

The correct Answer is D: 20.0 ÷ 2.5 = 8

How to Solve Word Problems

Most students find math word problems difficult. Tackling word problems is much easier if you have a systematic approach which we outline below.

Here is the biggest tip for studying word problems.

Practice regularly and systematically. Sounds simple and easy right? Yes it is, and yes it really does work.

Word problems are a way of thinking and require you to translate a real word problem into mathematical terms.

Some math instructors go so far as to say that learning how to think mathematically is the main reason for teaching word problems.

So what do we mean by Practice regularly and systematically? Studying word problems and math in general requires a logical and mathematical frame of mind. The only way you can get this is by practicing regularly, which means everyday.

It is critical that you practice word problems everyday for the 5 days before the exam as a bare minimum.

If you practice and miss a day, you have lost the mathematical frame of mind and the benefit of your previous practice is pretty much gone. Anyone who has done any amount of math will agree – you have to practice everyday.

Everything is important. The other critical point about word problems is that all the information given in the problem has some purpose. There is no unnecessary information! Word problems are typically around 50 words in 1 to 3 sentences. If the sometimes complicated relationships are to be explained in that short an explanation, every word has to count. Make sure that you use every piece of information.

Here are 9 simple steps to solve word problems.

Step 1 – Read through the problem at least three times. The first reading should be a quick scan, and the next two readings should be done slowly with a view to finding answers to these important questions:

What does the problem ask? (Usually located towards the end of the problem)

What does the problem imply? (This is usually a point you were asked to remember).

Mark all information, and underline all important words or phrases.

Step 2 – Try to make a pictorial representation of the problem such as a circle and an arrow to indicate travel. This makes the problem a bit more real and sensible to you.

A favorite word problem is something like, 1 train leaves Station A travelling at 100 km/hr and another train leaves Station B travelling at 60 km/hr. ...

Draw a line, the two stations, and the two trains at either end. This will help solidify the situation in your mind.

Step 3 – Use the information you have to make a table with a blank portion to indicate information you do not know.

Step 4 – Assign a single letter to represent each unknown data in your table. You can write down the unknown that each letter represents so that you do not make the error of assigning answers to the wrong unknown, because a word problem may have multiple unknowns and you will need to create equations for each unknown.

Step 5 – Translate the English terms in the word problem into a mathematical algebraic equation. Remember that the main problem with word problems is that they are not expressed in regular math equations. You ability to correctly identify the variables and translate the word problem into an equation determines your ability to solve the problem.

Step 6 – Check the equation to see if it looks like regular equations that you are used to seeing and whether it looks sensible. Does the equation appear to represent the information in the question? Take note that you may need to rewrite some formulas needed to solve the word problem equation. For example, word distance problems may need you rewriting the distance formula, which is Distance = Time x Rate. If the word problem requires that you solve for time you will need to use Distance/Rate and Distance/Time to solve for Rate. If you understand the distance word problem you should be able to identify the variable you need to solve for.

Step 7 – Use algebra rules to solve the derived equation. Take note that the laws of equation demands that what is done on this side of the equation has to also be done on the other side. You have to solve the equation so that the unknown ends up alone on one side. Where there are multiple unknowns you will need to use elimination or substitution methods to resolve all the equations.

Step 8 – Check your final answers to see if they make sense with the information given in the problem. For example if the word problem involves a discount, the final price should be less or if a product was taxed then the final answer has to cost more.

Step 9 – Cross check your answers by placing the answer or answers in the first equation to replace the unknown or unknowns. If your answer is correct then both side of the equation must equate or equal. If your answer is not correct then you may have derived a wrong equation or solved the equation wrongly. Repeat the necessary steps to correct.

Types of Word Problems

Word problems can be classified into 12 types. Below are examples of each type with a complete solution. Some types of word problems can be solved quickly using multiple choice strategies and some cannot. Always look for ways to estimate the answer and then eliminate choices.

1. Age

A girl is 10 years older than her brother. By next year, she will be twice the age of her brother. What are their ages now?

    a. 25, 15
    b. 19, 9
    c. 21, 11
    d. 29, 19

Solution: B

We will assume that the girl's age is "a" and her brother's is "b." This means that based on the information in the first sentence,
$a = 10 + b$

Next year, she will be twice her brother's age, which gives
$a + 1 = 2(b+1)$

We need to solve for one unknown factor and then use the answer to solve for the other. To do this we substitute the value of "a" from the first equation into the second equation. This gives

10+b + 1 = 2b + 2
11 + b = 2b + 2
11 − 2 = 2b − b
b= 9

9 = b this means that her brother is 9 years old. Solving for the girl's age in the first equation gives a = 10 + 9. a = 19 the girl is aged 19. So, the girl is aged 19 and the boy is 9

2. Distance or speed

Two boats travel down a river towards the same destination, starting at the same time. One boat is traveling at 52 km/hr, and the other boat at 43 km/hr. How far apart will they be after 40 minutes?

    a. 46.67 km
    b. 19.23 km
    c. 6.0 km
    d. 14.39 km

Solution: C

After 40 minutes, the first boat will have traveled = 52 km/hr x 40 minutes/60 minutes = 34.66 km
After 40 minutes, the second boat will have traveled = 43 km/hr x 40/60 minutes = 28.66 km
Difference between the two boats will be 34.66 km − 28.66 km = 6 km.

Multiple Choice Strategy

First estimate the answer. The first boat is travelling 9 km. faster than the second, for 40 minutes, which is 2/3 of an hour. 2/3 of 9 = 6, as a rough guess of the distance apart.

Choices A, B and D can be eliminated right away.

3. Ratio

The instructions in a cookbook states that 700 grams of

flour must be mixed in 100 ml of water, and 0.90 grams of salt added. A cook however has just 325 grams of flour. What is the quantity of water and salt that he should use?

    a. 0.41 grams and 46.4 ml
    b. 0.45 grams and 49.3 ml
    c. 0.39 grams and 39.8 ml
    d. 0.25 grams and 40.1 ml

Solution: A

The Cookbook states 700 grams of flour, but the cook only has 325. The first step is to determine the percentage of flour he has 325/700 x 100 = 46.4%
That means that 46.4% of all other items must also be used.
46.4% of 100 = 46.4 ml of water
46.4% of 0.90 = 0.41 grams of salt.

Multiple Choice Strategy

The recipe calls for 700 grams of flour but the cook only has 325, which is just less than half, the amount of water and salt are going to be about half.

Choices C and D can be eliminated right away. Choice B is very close so be careful. Looking closely at Choice B, it is exactly half, and since 325 is slightly less than half of 700, it can't be correct.

Choice A is correct.

4. Percent

An agent received $6,685 as his commission for selling a property. If his commission was 13% of the selling price, how much was the property?

    a. $68,825
    b. $121,850
    c. $49,025
    d. $51,423

Solution: D

Let's assume that the property price is x
That means from the information given, 13% of x = 6,685
Solve for x,
x = 6685 x 100/13 = $51,423

Multiple Choice Strategy

The commission, 13%, is just over 10%, which is easier to work with. Round up $6685 to $6700, and multiple by 10 for an approximate answer. 10 X 6700 = $67,000. You can do this in your head. Choice B is much too big and can be eliminated. Choice C is too small and can be eliminated. Choices A and D are left and good possibilities.

Do the calculations to make the final choice.

5. Sales & Profit

A store owner buys merchandise for $21,045. He transports them for $3,905 and pays his staff $1,450 to stock the merchandise on his shelves. If he does not incur further costs, how much does he need to sell the items to make $5,000 profit?

    a. $32,500
    b. $29,350
    c. $32,400
    d. $31,400

Solution: D

Total cost of the items is $21,045 + $3,905 + $1,450 = $26,400
Total cost is now $26,400 + $5000 profit = $31,400

Multiple Choice Strategy

Round off and add the numbers up in your head quickly. 21,000 + 4,000 + 1500 = 26500. Add in 5000 profit for a total of 31500.

Choice B is too small and can be eliminated. Choice C and Choice A are too large and can be eliminated.

6. Tax/Income

A woman earns $42,000 per month and pays 5% tax on her monthly income. If the Government increases her monthly taxes by $1,500, what is her income after tax?

    a. $38,400
    b. $36,050
    c. $40,500
    d. $39, 500

Solution: A

Initial tax on income was 5/100 x 42,000 = $2,100
$1,500 was added to the tax to give $2,100 + 1,500 = $3,600
Income after tax left is $42,000 - $3,600 = $38,400

7. Interest

A man invests $3000 in a 2-year term deposit that pays 3% interest per year. How much will he have at the end of the 2-year term?

    a. $5,200
    b. $3,020
    c. $3,182.7
    d. $3,000

Solution: C

This is a compound interest problem. The funds are invested for 2 years and interest is paid yearly, so in the second year, he will earn interest on the interest paid in the first year.

3% interest in the first year = 3/100 x 3,000 = $90
At end of first year, total amount = 3,000 + 90 = $3,090
Second year = 3/100 x 3,090 = 92.7.

At end of second year, total amount = $3090 + $92.7 = $3,182.7

8. Averaging

The average weight of 10 books is 54 grams. 2 more books were added and the average weight became 55.4. If one of the 2 new books added weighed 62.8 g, what is the weight of the other?

    a. 44.7 g
    b. 67.4 g
    c. 62 g
    d. 52 g

Solution: C

Total weight of 10 books with average 54 grams will be=10×54=540 g
Total weight of 12 books with average 55.4 will be=55.4×12=664.8 g
So total weight of the remaining 2 will be= 664.8 − 540 = 124.8 g
If one weighs 62.8, the weight of the other will be= 124.8 g − 62.8 g = 62 g

Multiple Choice Strategy

Averaging problems can be estimated by looking at which direction the average goes. If additional items are added and the average goes up, the new items much be greater than the average. If the average goes down after new items are added, the new items must be less than the average.

In this case, the average is 54 grams and 2 books are added which increases the average to 55.4, so the new books must weight more than 54 grams.

Choices A and D can be eliminated right away.

9. Probability

A bag contains 15 marbles of various colors. If 3 marbles are white, 5 are red and the rest are black, what is the probability of randomly picking out a black marble from the bag?

    a. 7/15
    b. 3/15
    c. 1/5
    d. 4/15

Solution: A

Total marbles = 15
Number of black marbles = 15 − (3 + 5) = 7
Probability of picking out a black marble = 7/15

10. Two Variables

A company paid a total of $2850 to book for 6 single rooms and 4 double rooms in a hotel for one night. Another company paid $3185 to book for 13 single rooms for one night in the same hotel. What is the cost for single and double rooms in that hotel?

    a. single= $250 and double = $345
    b. single= $254 and double = $350
    c. single = $245 and double = $305
    d. single = $245 and double = $345

Solution: D

We can determine the price of single rooms from the information given of the second company. 13 single rooms = 3185.
One single room = 3185 / 13 = 245
The first company paid for 6 single rooms at $245. 245 x 6 = $1470
Total amount paid for 4 double rooms by first company = $2850 - $1470 = $1380
Cost per double room = 1380 / 4 = $345

11. Geometry

The length of a rectangle is 5 in. more than its width. The perimeter of the rectangle is 26 in. What is the width and length of the rectangle?

    a. width = 6 inches, Length = 9 inches
    b. width = 4 inches, Length = 9 inches
    c. width =4 inches, Length = 5 inches
    d. width = 6 inches, Length = 11 inches

Solution: B

Formula for perimeter of a rectangle is 2(L + W)
p=26, so 2(L+W) = p
The length is 5 inches more than the width, so
2(w+5) + 2w = 26
2w + 10 + 2w = 26
2w + 2w = 26 - 10
4w = 16

W = 16/4 = 4 inches

L is 5 inches more than w, so L = 5 + 4 = 9 inches.

12. Totals and fractions

A basket contains 125 oranges, mangos and apples. If 3/5 of the fruits in the basket are mangos and only 2/5 of the mangos are ripe, how many ripe mangos are there in the basket?

    a. 30
    b. 68
    c. 55
    d. 47

Solution: A
Number of mangos in the basket is 3/5 x 125 = 75
Number of ripe mangos = 2/5 x 75 = 30

Order Of Operation

Some math calculations contain more than one set of operations. For example, a problem like 3 + (35 - 21) x 2 requires addition, subtraction and multiplication operations. The problem arises from the confusion of which of the operations to perform first. Starting with the wrong operation will give you the wrong answer. To solve this dilemma and to avoid confusion, the Order of Operation rules were set.

Order of operation is a set of mathematical rules designed to be used for calculations that require more than one arithmetic operation. For example, calculation problems that require two or more out of addition, subtraction, multiplication and division, would require that you follow the order of operation to solve.

The order of operation rules are quite simple as explained below.

> **Rule 1:** Start with calculations that are inside brackets or parentheses.
> **Rule 2:** Then, solve all multiplications and divisions, from left to right.
> **Rule 3:** Finally, solve all additions and subtractions, from left to right.

Example 1

Solve 16 + 5 x 8

Based on the rules above, we would have to start with the multiplication part of the question.
That will give: 16 + 40 = 56

Take note that if the rule was not followed and addition was done first, the answer gotten would be different and wrong.

16 + 5 x 8
21 x 8 = 168 (wrong answer)

Example 2

3 +(35 - 21) x 2

Based on the rules of the order of operation, we have to solve the problem in the bracket or parenthesis first. Then we do the multiplication, before doing the addition.

3 + (35 - 21) x 2
3 + (14) x 3
3 + 42
= 45

Scientific Notation

Science notation is a very simple and effective way of representing very large numbers in simpler forms. For example, instead of writing out 149,600,000,000 meters, which is the estimated distance from the sun, astronomers could easily write it out as 1.496×10^{11} meters.
Scientific notation expresses numbers in their powers of ten. It can be used to even express simple numbers.
For example, using scientific notation, $10 = 10^1$ The exponent "1" tell the number of times to multiply by 10 to get the original number.
$100 = 10^2$
$1000 = 10^3$
$100 = 1$

When the exponent is negative, it tells us how many times we need to divide by ten to get the original number.

For example, $0.025 = 2.5 \times 10$

The accepted format of scientific notation or writing numbers on their powers of 10 is $a \times 10^n$
Where a must be between 1 and 10 and n must be an integer

How to convert to scientific notation

To convert a number to scientific notation, you would need to place a decimal after the first number that is not a zero or after the first number that ranges between 1 and 9.

After placing the decimal, you need to count the number of places that the decimal had to move to get the exponent of 10. If the decimal moves to the left, then the exponent to multiply 10 will be in the positive. If the decimal moves from right to left, we will then have a negative power of 10.

For example, to convert 29010, we need to place a decimal after 2, since 2 is the first non zero number. We would then have 2.91

If we were to convert 0.0167, we need to place the decimal after 1, since the first two numbers before 1 were zeros and do not fall between 1 and 9. We would thus have 1.67

To complete the conversion of 29010 to scientific notation, we would get 2.91×10^4

The 10 is raised to the power of 4, because there are 4 places counting from the right to left where the decimal had to move. This scientific notation is in the positive because the decimal moved to the left.

$0.0167 = 1.67 \times 10^{-2}$

In this example, the decimal place moved from left to right by 2 spaces thus the 10 is raised to the power of 2. It is in the negative, because the decimal moved towards the right.

How to convert from scientific notation

You may also need to convert numbers that are already represented in scientific notation or in their power of ten to regular numbers. It is quite easy.

First it is important to remember these two laws.

If the power is in the positive, shift decimal to the right
If the power is in the negative, shift decimal point to the left

Example

Convert 3.201×10^3

This scientific notation is in the positive so we just need to shift the decimal to the right by 2 spaces, which is the power of the 10. We thus have: $3.201 \times 10^3 = 3201$

Another example

Convert

1.03×10^{-4}

The scientific notation here is negative and so we need to shift decimal to the left. Thus $1.03 \times 10^{-4} = 0.000103$ The decimal was shifted 4 spaces to the left.

Ratios

In mathematics, a ratio is a relationship between two numbers of the same kind[1] (e.g., objects, persons, students, spoonfuls, units of whatever identical dimension), usually expressed as "a to b" or a:b, sometimes expressed arithmetically as a dimensionless quotient of the two[2] which explicitly indicates how many times the first number contains the second (not necessarily an integer).[3] In layman's terms a ratio represents, simply, for every amount of one thing, how much there is of another thing. For example, suppose I have 10 pairs of socks for every pair of shoes then the ratio of shoes:socks would be 1:10 and the ratio of socks:shoes would be 10:1.

Notation and terminology

The ratio of numbers A and B can be expressed as:[4]
the ratio of A to B
A is to B
A:B

A rational number which is the quotient of A divided by B
The numbers A and B are sometimes called terms with A being the antecedent and B being the consequent.

The proportion expressing the equality of the ratios A:B and C:D is written A:B=C:D or A:B::C:D. this latter form, when spoken or written in the English language, is often expressed as
A is to B as C is to D.

Again, A, B, C, D are called the terms of the proportion. A and D are called the extremes, and B and C are called the means. The equality of three or more proportions is called a continued proportion.[5]
Ratios are sometimes used with three or more terms. The dimensions of a two by four that is ten inches long are 2:4:10.

Examples

The quantities being compared in a ratio might be physical quantities such as speed or length, or numbers of objects, or amounts of particular substances. A common example of the last case is the weight ratio of water to cement used in concrete, which is commonly stated as 1:4. This means that the weight of cement used is four times the weight of water used. It does not say anything about the total amounts of cement and water used, nor the amount of concrete being made. Equivalently it could be said that the ratio of cement to water is 4:1, that there is 4 times as much cement as water, or that there is a quarter (1/4) as much water as cement..
Older televisions have a 4:3 "aspect ratio," which means that the width is 4/3 of the height; modern widescreen TVs have a 16:9 aspect ratio.

Fractional

If there are 2 oranges and 3 apples, the ratio of oranges to apples is 2:3, and the ratio of oranges to the total number of pieces of fruit is 2:5. These ratios can also be expressed in fraction form: there are 2/3 as many oranges as apples, and 2/5 of the pieces of fruit are oranges. If orange juice concentrate is to be diluted with water in the ratio 1:4, then one part of concentrate is mixed with four parts of water, giving five parts total; the amount of orange juice concentrate is 1/4 the amount of water, while the amount of orange juice concentrate is 1/5 of the total liquid. In both ratios and fractions, it is important to be clear what is being compared to what, and beginners often make mistakes for this reason.

Number of terms

In general, when comparing the quantities of a two-quantity ratio, this can be expressed as a fraction derived from the ratio. For example, in a ratio of 2:3, the amount/size/volume/number of the first quantity will be that of the second quantity. This pattern also works with ratios with more than two terms. However, a ratio with more than two terms cannot be completely converted into a single fraction; a single fraction represents only one part of the ratio since a fraction can only compare two numbers. If the ratio deals with objects or amounts of objects, this is often expressed as "for every two parts of the first quantity there are three parts of the second quantity."

Percent and ratio

If we multiply all quantities involved in a ratio by the same number, the ratio remains valid. For example, a ratio of 3:2 is the same as 12:8. It is usual either to reduce terms to the lowest common denominator, or to express them in parts per hundred (percent).

If a mixture contains substances A, B, C & D in the ratio 5:9:4:2 then there are 5 parts of A for every 9 parts of B, 4 parts of C and 2 parts of D. As 5+9+4+2=20, the total mixture contains 5/20 of A (5 parts out of 20), 9/20 of B, 4/20 of C, and 2/20 of D. If we divide all numbers by the total and multiply by 100, this is converted to percentages: 25% A, 45% B, 20% C, and 10% D (equivalent to writing the ratio as 25:45:20:10).

Proportion

If the two or more ratio quantities encompass all of the quantities in a particular situation, for example two apples and three oranges in a fruit basket containing no other types of fruit, it could be said that "the whole" contains five parts, made up of two parts apples and three parts oranges. In this case, or 40% of the whole are apples or 60% of the whole are oranges. This comparison of a specific quantity to "the whole" is sometimes called a proportion. Proportions are sometimes expressed as percentages as demonstrated above.

Reduction

Note that ratios can be reduced (as fractions are) by dividing each quantity by the common factors of all the quantities. This is often called "cancelling." As for fractions, the simplest form is considered to be that in which the numbers in the ratio are the smallest possible integers.

Thus, the ratio 40:60 may be considered equivalent in meaning to the ratio 2:3 within contexts concerned only with relative quantities.

Mathematically, we write: "40:60" = "2:3" (dividing both quantities by 20).
Grammatically, we would say, "40 to 60 equals 2 to 3."
An alternative representation is: "40:60::2:3"
Grammatically, we would say, "40 is to 60 as 2 is to 3."
A ratio that has integers for both quantities and that cannot be reduced any further (using integers) is said to be in simplest form or lowest terms.
Sometimes it is useful to write a ratio in the form 1:n or n:1 to enable comparisons of different ratios.

For example, the ratio 4:5 can be written as 1:1.25 (dividing both sides by 4). Alternatively, 4:5 can be written as 0.8:1 (dividing both sides by 5). Where the context makes the meaning clear, a ratio in this form is sometimes written without the 1 and the colon, though, mathematically, this makes it a factor or multiplier. [11]

Cartesian Plane, Coordinate Plane and Coordinate Grid

To locate dots and draw lines and curves, we use the coordinate plane. It also called Cartesian coordinate plane. It is a two-dimensional surface with a coordinate grid in it, which helps us to count the units. For the counting of those units, we use x-axis (horizontal scale) and y-axis (vertical scale).

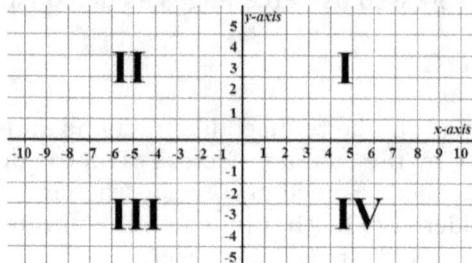

The whole system is called a coordinate system which is divided into 4 parts, called quadrants. The quadrant where all numbers are positive is the 1st quadrant (I), and if we go counterclockwise, we mark all 4 quadrants.

The location of a dot in the coordinate system is represented by coordinates. Coordinates are represented as a pair of numbers, where the 1st number is located on the x-axis and the 2nd number is located on the y-axis. So, if a dot A has coordinates a and b, then we write:

A=(a,b)   or   A(a,b)

The point where x-axis and y-axis intersect is called an origin. The origin is the point from which we measure the distance along the x and y axes.

In the Cartesian coordinate system we can calculate the distance between 2 given points. If we have dots with coordinates:
A=(a,b)
B=(c,d)

Then the distance d between A and B can be calculated by the following formula:

$$d = \sqrt{(c-a)^2 + (d-b)^2}$$

Cartesian coordinate system is used for the drawing of 2-dimentional shapes, and is also commonly used for functions.
Example:

Draw the function   y = (1 - x)/2

To draw a linear function, we need at least 2 points.
If we put that x=0 then value for y would be:

$$y = \frac{1-x}{2} = \frac{1-0}{2} = \frac{1}{2}$$

We found the 1st point, let's name it A, with following coordinates:

A = (0,1/2)

To find the 2nd point, we can put that x=1. In this case, the value for y would be:

$$y = \frac{1-x}{2} = \frac{1-1}{2} = \frac{0}{2} = 0$$

If we denote the 2nd point with B, then the coordinates for this point are:

B=(1,0)

Since we have 2 points necessary for the function, we find them in the coordinate system and we connect them with a line that represents the function,

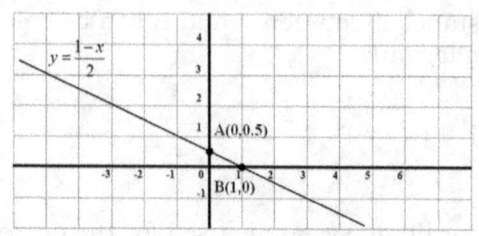

Perimeter Area and Volume

Perimeter and Area (2-dimentional shapes)

Perimeter of a shape determines the length around that shape, while the area includes the space inside the shape.

Rectangle:

$P = 2a + 2b$
$A = ab$

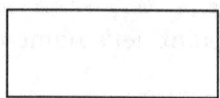

Square

$P = 4a$
$A = a^2$

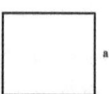

Parallelogram

$P = 2a + 2b$
$A = ah_a = bh_b$

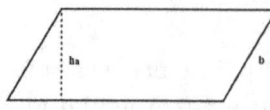

Rhombus

$P = 4a$

$A = ah = \dfrac{d_1 d_2}{2}$

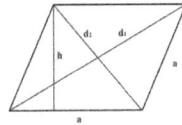

Triangle

$P = a+b+c$

$A = \dfrac{ah_a}{2} = \dfrac{bh_b}{2} = \dfrac{ch_c}{2}$

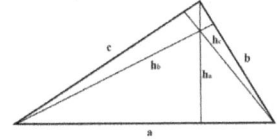

Equilateral Triangle

$P = 3a$

$A = \dfrac{a^2 \sqrt{3}}{4}$

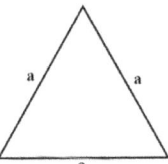

Trapezoid

$P = a+b+c+d$

$A = \dfrac{a+b}{2} h$

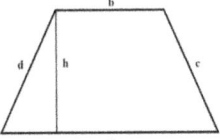

Circle

$P = 2r\pi$

$A = r^2 \pi$

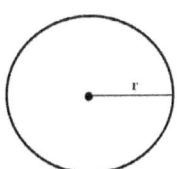

Area and Volume (3-dimentional shapes)

To calculate the area of a 3-dimentional shape, we calculate the areas of all sides and then we add them all.

To find the volume of a 3-dimentional shape, we multiply the area of the base (B) and the height (H) of the 3-dimentional shape.

$$V = BH$$

In case of a pyramid and a cone, the volume would be divided by 3.

$$V = BH/3$$

Here are some of the 3-dimentional shapes with formulas for their area and volume:

Cuboids

$A = 2(ab + bc + ac)$
$V = abc$

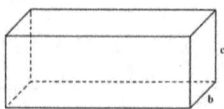

Cube

$A = 6a^2$
$V = a^3$

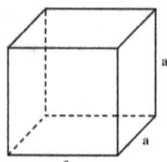

Pyramid

$A = ab + ah_a + bh_b$
$V = \dfrac{abH}{3}$

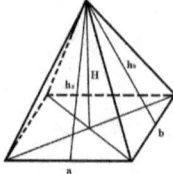

Cylinder

$$A = 2r^2\pi + 2r\pi H$$
$$V = r^2\pi H$$

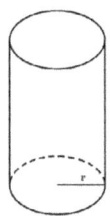

Cone

$$A = (r+s)r\pi$$
$$V = \frac{r^2\pi H}{3}$$

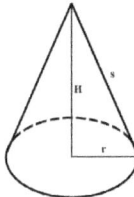

Pythagorean Geometry

If we have a right triangle ABC, where its sides (legs) are a and b and c is a hypotenuse (the side opposite the right angle), then we can establish a relationship between these sides using the following formula:

$$c^2 = a^2 + b^2$$

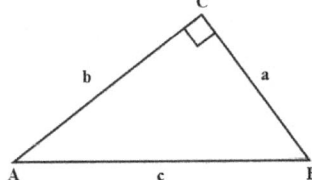

This formula is proven in the Pythagorean Theorem. There are many proofs of this theorem, but we'll look at just one geometrical proof:

If we draw squares on the right triangle's sides, then the area of the square on the hypotenuse is equal to the sum of the areas of the squares that are on other two sides of the triangle. Since the areas of these squares are a², b² and c², that is how we got the formula above.

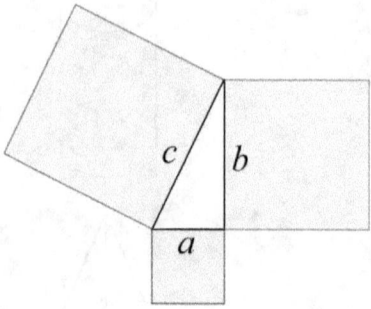

One of the famous right triangles is one with sides 3, 4 and 5. And we can see here that:

$3^2 + 4^2 = 5^2$
$9 + 16 = 25$
$25 = 25$

Example Problem:

The isosceles triangle ABC has a perimeter of 18 centimeters, and the difference between its base and legs is 3 centimeters. Find the height of this triangle.

We write the information we have about triangle ABC and we draw a picture of it for better understanding of the relation

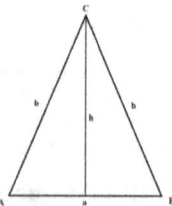

between its elements:

P=18 cm
a - b = 3 cm
h=?

We use the formula for the perimeter of the isosceles triangle, since that is what is given to us:

P = a + 2b = 18 cm

Notice that we have 2 equations with 2 variables, so we can solve it as a system of equations:

a + 2b = 18
a − b = 3 / a + 2b = 18
2a − 2b = 6 / a + 2b + 2a − 2b = 18 + 6
3a = 24
a = 24/3 = 8 cm

Now we go back to find b:
a − b = 3
8 − b = 3
b = 8 − 3
b = 5 cm

Using Pythagorean Theorem, we can find the height using a and b, because the height falls on the side a at the right angle. Notice that height cuts side a exactly in half, and that's why we use in the formula a/2. In this case, b is our hypotenuse, so we have:

$b^2 = (a/2)^2 + h^2$
$h^2 = b^2 - (a/2)^2$
$h^2 = 5^2 - (8/2)^2$
$h^2 = 5^2 - (8/2)^2$
$h^2 = 25 - 4^2$
$h^2 = 26 - 16$
$h^2 = 9$
h = 3 cm.

Congruence

Two geometrical shapes are congruent if their elements (sides and angles) are equal, but they don't have to have the same direction. So, here we are only interested in the size and shapes. For example, angles α and β are congruent if they have the same size, but not necessarily the same direction:

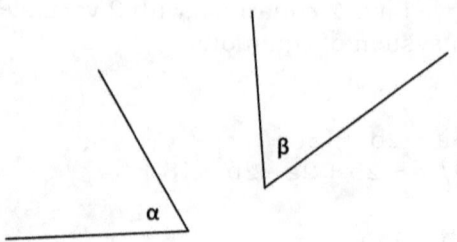

We write the congruence like this: $a \cong \beta \; a \cong \beta$
We can also say that 2 triangles are congruent if their appropriate elements are equal:

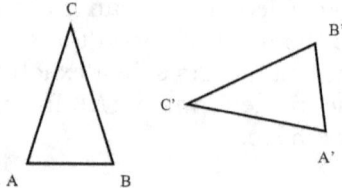

So, we write: $ABC \cong A'B'C'$

The most important congruence rules are concerning triangles, and they are used for congruence of almost all 2D shapes (quadrilaterals, hexagons etc). There are 4 rules:

1. Side-Angle-Side (SAS)
If 2 triangles have 2 equal sides and an equal angles that are between those sides, then we can conclude that these 2 triangles are congruent.

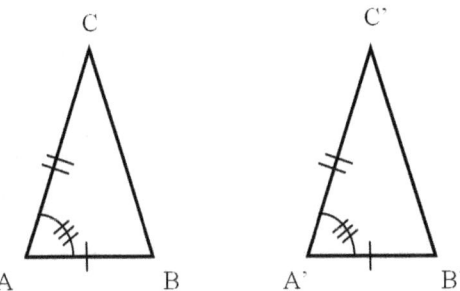

2. Side-Side-Side (SSS)
If 2 triangles have all 3 sides that are equal, then these 2 triangles are congruent.

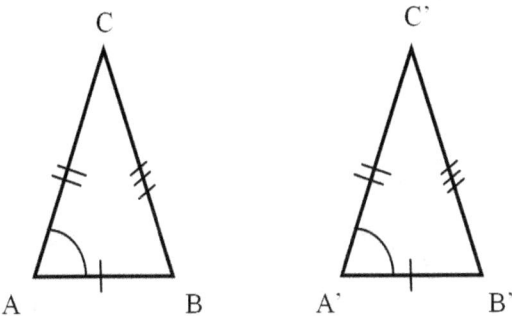

3. Angle-Side-Angle (ASA)
If 2 triangles have 2 equal angles and an equal side that is between them, then these 2 triangles are congruent.

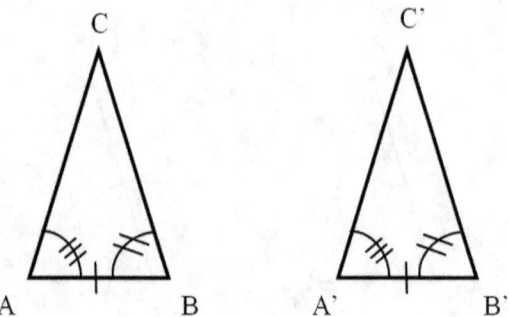

4. Side-Side-Angle (SSA)
If 2 triangles have 2 equal sides, and an equal angle that is not between those 2 sides, then these 2 triangles are congruent.

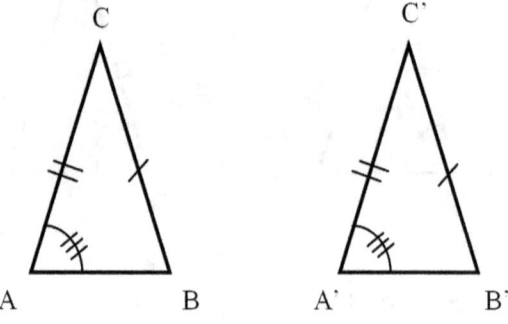

Let's look at an example question.

Consider the 2 triangles ABC and A'B'C'.
We see that we have a case of SAS:

So we can conclude that triangles ABC and A'B'C' are congruent. So, we write:

ABC ≅ A'B'C'

Quadrilaterals

Quadrilaterals are 2-dimentional geometrical shapes that have 4 sides and 4 angles. There are many types of quadrilaterals, depending on the length of its sides and if they are parallel and also depending on the size of its angles. All quadrilaterals have the following properties:

>Sum of all interior angles is 360^0

>Sum of all exterior angles is 360^0

A quadrilateral is a parallelogram is it fulfills at least one of the following conditions:

>Angles on each side are supplementary
>Opposite angles are equal
>Opposite sides are equal
>Diagonals intersect each other exactly in half

Here are some of the quadrilaterals:

Square

All sides are equal
All angles are right angles

Rectangle

2 pairs of equal sides
All angles are right angles

Parallelogram

2 pairs of equal sides
Opposite angles are equal

Rhombus

All sides are equal
Opposite angles are equal

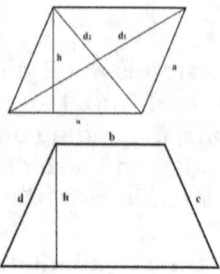

Trapezoid

One pair of parallel sides

Example Problem
Find all angles of a parallelogram if one angle is greater than the other one by $40°$.

First, we draw an image of a parallelogram:

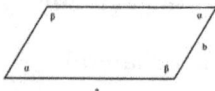

We denote angles by α and β, Since this is a parallelogram, the opposite angles are equal.

We are given that one angle is greater than the other one by $40°$, so we can write:

$\beta = \alpha + 40°$

We solve this problem in two ways:
1) The sum of all internal angles of every quadrilateral is $360°$. There are 2 α and 2 β. So we have:
$2\alpha + 2\beta = 360°$

Now, instead of β we write α + 40:
$2\alpha + 2(\alpha + 40°) = 360°$
$2\alpha + 2\alpha + 80° = 360°$
$4\alpha = 360° - 80°$

$4α = 280°$
$α = 280° / 4$
$α = 70°$
Now we can find β from α:
$β = α + 40°$
$β = 70° + 40°$
$β = 110°$

2) One condition for parallelogram is " Angles on each side are supplementary" and we can use that to find these angles:
$α + β = 180°$
$α + α + 40° = 180°$
$2α = 180° - 40°$
$2α = 140°$
$α = 70°$

Now we find β:
$β = α + 40°$
$β = 70° + 40°$
$β = 110°$

Solving One-Variable Linear Equations

Linear equations with variable x is an equation with the following form:
$$ax = b$$
where a and b are real numbers. If a=0 and b is different from 0, then the equation has no solution.

Let's solve one simple example of a linear equation with one variable:
$$4x - 2 = 2x + 6$$

When we are given this type of equation, we are always moving variables to the one side, and real numbers to the other side of the equals sign. Always remember: if you are changing sides, you are changing signs. Let's move all variables to the left, and real number to the right side:

$4x - 2 = 2x + 6$
$4x - 2x = 6 + 2$
$2x = 8$
$x = 8:2$
$x = 4$

When 2x goes to the left it becomes -2x, and -2 goes to the right and becomes +2. After calculations, we find that x is 4, which is a solution of our linear equation.

Let's solve a little more complex linear equation:

$2x - 6/4 + 4 = x$
$2x - 6 + 16 = 4x$
$2x - 4x = -16 + 6$
$-2x = -10$
$x = -10/-2$
$x = 5$

We multiply whole equation by 4, to lose the fractional line. Now we have a simple linear equation. If we change sides, we change the signs.

Solving Two-Variable Linear Equations

If we have 2 or more linear equations with 2 or more variables, then we have a system of linear equations. The idea here is to express one variable using the other in one equation, and then use it in the second equation, so we get a linear equation with one variable. Here is an example:

$x - y = 3$
$2x + y = 9$

From the first equation, we express y using x.

$y = x - 3$

In the second equation, we write x-3 instead of y. And there we get a linear equation with one variable x.

2x + x - 3 = 9
3x = 9 + 3
3x = 12
x = 12/3
x = 4

Now that we found x, we can use it to find y.

y = x - 3
y = 4 - 3
y = 1

So, the solution of this system is (x,y) = (4,1).

Let's solve one more system using a different method:

Solve:

5x - 3y = 17
x + 3y = 11

5x - 3y + x + 3y = 17 - 11

Notice that we have -3y in the first equation and +3y in the second. If we add these 2, we get zero, which means we lose variable y. So, we add these 2 equations and we get a linear equation with one variable.

6x = 6
x = 1

Now that we have x, we use it to find y.

5 - 3y = 17
-3y = 17 - 5
-3y = 12
y = 12/(-3)
y = -4

English Language Arts

THIS SECTION CONTAINS AN ENGLISH LANGUAGE ARTS SELF-ASSESSMENT. The tutorials are designed to familiarize general principles and the self-assessment contains general questions similar to the essay revision questions likely to be on the CAHSEE exam, but are not intended to be identical to the exam questions. The tutorials are not designed to be a complete course, and it is assumed that students have some familiarity with English grammar and usage. If you do not understand parts of the tutorial, or find the tutorial difficult, it is recommended that you seek out additional instruction.

Tour of the CAHSEE English Language Arts Content

The CAHSEE English Language Arts section has three parts, basic grammar, essay revisions, and an essay. How to write an essay is a big topic and covered in the next chapter. There are 15 grammar questions and 12 essay revision questions. Below is a detailed list of the topics likely to appear on the CAHSEE.

- Identify sentence fragments

- Main idea

- Redundancy

- Punctuation

- English Usage

- English Grammar

- Punctuation

The questions in the self-assessment are not the same as you will find on the CAHSEE - that would be too easy! And nobody knows what the questions will be and they change all the time. Mostly, the changes consist of substituting new questions for old, but the changes also can be new question formats or styles, changes to the number of questions in each section, changes to the time limits for each section, and combining sections. So, while the format and exact wording of the questions may differ slightly, and changes from year to year, if you can answer the questions below, you will have no problem with the English Language Arts section of the CAHSEE.

English Language Arts Self-Assessment - Part 1

The purpose of the self-assessment is:

- Identify your strengths and weaknesses.

- Develop your personalized study plan (above)

- Get accustomed to the CAHSEE format

- Extra practice – the self-assessments are almost a full 3rd practice test!

- Provide a baseline score for preparing your study schedule.

Since this is a Self-assessment, and depending on how confident you are with essay revision, timing yourself is optional. The CAHSEE has 25 questions, to be answered in 30 minutes. This self-assessment has 25 questions, so allow 30 minutes to complete.

English Language Arts Self-Assessment

1. Ⓐ Ⓑ Ⓒ Ⓓ   11. Ⓐ Ⓑ Ⓒ Ⓓ   21. Ⓐ Ⓑ Ⓒ Ⓓ
2. Ⓐ Ⓑ Ⓒ Ⓓ   12. Ⓐ Ⓑ Ⓒ Ⓓ   22. Ⓐ Ⓑ Ⓒ Ⓓ
3. Ⓐ Ⓑ Ⓒ Ⓓ   13. Ⓐ Ⓑ Ⓒ Ⓓ   23. Ⓐ Ⓑ Ⓒ Ⓓ
4. Ⓐ Ⓑ Ⓒ Ⓓ   14. Ⓐ Ⓑ Ⓒ Ⓓ   24. Ⓐ Ⓑ Ⓒ Ⓓ
5. Ⓐ Ⓑ Ⓒ Ⓓ   15. Ⓐ Ⓑ Ⓒ Ⓓ   25. Ⓐ Ⓑ Ⓒ Ⓓ
6. Ⓐ Ⓑ Ⓒ Ⓓ   16. Ⓐ Ⓑ Ⓒ Ⓓ
7. Ⓐ Ⓑ Ⓒ Ⓓ   17. Ⓐ Ⓑ Ⓒ Ⓓ
8. Ⓐ Ⓑ Ⓒ Ⓓ   18. Ⓐ Ⓑ Ⓒ Ⓓ
9. Ⓐ Ⓑ Ⓒ Ⓓ   19. Ⓐ Ⓑ Ⓒ Ⓓ
10. Ⓐ Ⓑ Ⓒ Ⓓ   20. Ⓐ Ⓑ Ⓒ Ⓓ

Part 1 - Punctuation

1. Ted and Janice <u>who had been friends for years went on vacation together</u> every summer.

    a. Ted and Janice, who had been friends for years, went on vacation together every summer.

    b. Ted and Janice who had been friends for years, went on vacation together every summer.

    c. Ted, and Janice who had been friends for years, went on vacation together every summer.

    d. None of the choices are correct.

2. None of us want to go to the <u>party not even</u> if there will be live music.

    a. None of us want to go to the party not even, if there will be live music.

    b. None of us want to go to the party, not even if there will be live music.

    c. None of us want to go to the party; not even if there will be live music.

    d. None of the choice are correct.

3. <u>John, Maurice, and Thomas,</u> quit school two months before graduation.

    a. John, Maurice, and Thomas quit school two months before graduation.

    b. John, Maurice and Thomas quit school two months before graduation.

    c. John Maurice and Thomas, quit school two months before graduation.

    d. None of the choice are correct.

4. "My father said that he would be there on <u>Sunday,"</u> <u>Lee</u> explained.

a. "My father said that he would be there on Sunday" Lee explained.

b. None of the choices are correct.

c. "My father said that he would be there on Sunday," Lee explained.

d. "My father said that he would be there on Sunday." Lee explained.

5. I own two<u> dogs, a cat, named Jeffrey and Henry, the goldfish.</u>

a. I own two dogs, a cat named Jeffrey, and Henry, the goldfish.

b. I own two dogs a cat, named Jeffrey, and Henry, the goldfish.

c. I own two dogs, a cat named Jeffrey; and Henry, the goldfish.

d. None of the choices are correct.

6. Choose the sentence below with the correct punctuation.

a. Marcus who won the debate tournament, is the best speaker that I know.
b. Marcus, who won the debate tournament, is the best speaker that I know.
c. Marcus who won the debate tournament is the best speaker that I know.
d. Marcus who won the debate tournament is the best speaker, that I know.

Part II - Sentence Structure and Grammar

Combine the sentences below into one sentence with the same meaning.

7. I hate needles. I want to give blood. I can't give blood.

    a. Although I hate needles, I couldn't give blood even if I wanted to.
    b. Because I hate needles, I can't give blood, although I want to give blood.
    c. Whenever I hate needles, I give blood although I can't give blood.
    d. Whenever I can't give blood, I give blood anyway, although I hate needles.

8. The doctor was not looking forward to meeting Mrs. Lucas. The doctor would have to tell Mrs. Lucas that she has cancer. The doctor hates giving bad news to patients.

    a. The doctor hates giving bad news, so he was not looking forward to meeting Mrs. Lucas and telling her she has cancer.
    b. The doctor has cancer and was not looking forward to meeting Mrs. Lucas and telling her the bad news.
    c. Before the doctor met Mrs. Lucas, he had to give his the patients the bad news that Mrs. Lucas has cancer.
    d. The doctor was not looking forward to giving the bad news to his patients that he had to tell Mrs. Lucas that his patients have cancer.

9. Mom hates shopping. We were out of bread, milk and eggs. Mom went to the supermarket.

>a. Because we were out of bread, milk and eggs, Mom hated shopping at the supermarket.
>b. Although she hates shopping, Mom went to the supermarket since we were out of bread, milk and eggs.
>c. Although we were out of bread, milk and eggs, Mom still hated shopping at the supermarket and went there anyway.
>d. Because Mom hated shopping at the supermarket, she went to there to buy her bread, milk and eggs.

10. The ceremony had an emotional <u>affect</u> on the groom, but the bride was not <u>affected</u>.

>a. The ceremony had an emotional effect on the groom, but the bride was not affected.
>
>b. The ceremony had an emotional affect on the groom, but the bride was not affected.
>
>c. The ceremony had an emotional effect on the groom, but the bride was not effected.

11. Anna was taller <u>than Luis, but then</u> he grew four inches in three months.

>a. None of the choices are correct.
>b. Anna was taller then Luis, but than he grew four inches in three months.
>c. Anna was taller than Luis, but than he grew four inches, in three months.
>d. Anna was taller than Luis, but then he grew four inches in three months.

12. **There** second home is in Boca Raton, but **they're** not **there** for most of the year.

>a. Their second home is in Boca Raton, but there not their for most of the year.
>
>b. They're second home is in Boca Raton, but they're not there for most of the year.
>
>c. Their second home is in Boca Raton, but they're not there for most of the year.
>
>d. None of the choices are correct.

13. **Their** going to graduate in June; after that, **their** best option will be to go **there.**

>a. They're going to graduate in June; after that, their best option will be to go there.
>
>b. There going to graduate in June; after that, their best option will be to go there.
>
>c. They're going to graduate in June; after that, there best option will be to go their.
>
>d. None of the choices are correct.

14. **Your mistaken; that is not you're book.**

>a. You're mistaken; that is not you're book.
>
>b. Your mistaken; that is not your book.
>
>c. You're mistaken; that is not your book.
>
>d. None of the choices are correct.

15. **You're classes are on the west side of campus, but you're living on the east side.**

   a. You're classes are on the west side of campus, but you're living on the east side.

   b. Your classes are on the west side of campus, but your living on the east side.

   c. Your classes are on the west side of campus, but you're living on the east side.

   d. None of the choices are correct.

16. **The Chinese lives in one of the world's populous nations, while a citizen of Bermuda lives in one of the least populous.**

   a. The Chinese live in one of the world's most populous nations, while a citizen of Bermuda lives in one of the least populous.

   b. The Chinese lives in one of the world's most populous nations, while a citizen of Bermuda live in one of the least populous.

   c. The Chinese live in one of the world's most populous nations, while a citizen of Bermuda live in one of the least populous.

   d. None of the choices are correct.

17. **You shouldn't sit in that chair wearing black pants; I sit the white cat there just a moment ago.**

   a. You shouldn't sit in that chair wearing black pants; I set the white cat there just a moment ago.

   b. You shouldn't set in that chair wearing black pants; I sit the white cat there just a moment ago.

   c. You shouldn't set in that chair wearing black pants; I set the white cat there just a moment ago.

   d. None of the choices are correct.

18. We saw the <u>golden gate Bridge in San Francisco.</u>

   a. Golden Gate Bridge in San Francisco
   b. golden gate bridge in San Francisco
   c. Golden gate bridge in San Francisco
   d. None of the choice are correct.

Part III - Sentence Completion and Correction

19. Collecting stamps, _____ and listening to shortwave radio were Rick's main hobbies.

   a. building models
   b. to build models
   c. having built models
   d. build models

20. Every morning, _____, and before the sun comes up, my mother makes herself a cup of cocoa.

   a. after the kids left for school
   b. after the kids leave for school
   c. after the kids have left for school
   d. after the kids will leave for school

21. Elaine promised to bring the camera _____ at the mall yesterday.

   a. by me
   b. with me
   c. at me
   d. to me

22. Following the tornado, telephone poles _____ all over the street.

    a. laid
    b. lied
    c. were lying
    d. were laying

Part IV - Grammar – Sentence Correction

23. She is the <u>**most cleverest**</u> girl in the class.

    a. She is the most clever girl in the class.
    b. She is the cleverest girl in the class.
    c. She is the most cleverer girl in the class.
    d. None of the above.

24. He <u>**lived**</u> in California since 1995.

    a. He had lived in California since 1995.
    b. He has been living in California since 1995.
    c. He has living in California since 1995.
    d. None of the above.

25. Please excuse <u>**me being**</u> late.

    a. Please excuse me for late.
    b. Please excuse my being late.
    c. Please excuse my being lateness.
    d. None of the above.

English Self-Assessment Answer Key

1. A
Use a comma to separate phrases.

2. B
Use a comma separates independent clauses. None of us wants to go to the party, not even if there will be live music.

3. B
Don't use a comma before 'and' in a list.

4. C
Commas always go with a quote and the use of said, explained etc.

5. A
This is an example if a comma which appears before 'and,' but is disambiguating. Without the comma, the sentence would be "I own two dogs, a cat named Jeffrey and Henry, the goldfish." This means there is a cat named Jeffrey and Henry, and a goldfish with no name mentioned. The comma appears to show the distinction.

I own two dogs, a cat named Jeffrey, and Henry, the goldfish.

6. B
Comma separate phrases.

7. A
These three sentences can be combined using 'although,' and 'even if.'

8. A
These two sentences can be combined into one sentence with two clauses separated by a comma.

9. B
These three sentences can be combined using 'although,' and 'since.'

English Usage

10. A
Affect vs. Effect - Affect is a verb (action) and effect is a noun (thing).

11. D
Than vs. Then – Than is used for comparison, as in, taller than, and then is used for time, as in, but then...

12. C
There vs. their vs. they're. There indicates existence as in, "there are." Their is to indicate possession, as in, "their book." They're is the contraction form of "they are."

13. A
There vs. their vs. they're. There indicates existence as in, "there are." Their is to indicate possession, as in, "their book." They're is the contraction form of "they are."

14. C
Your vs. you're. Your is the possessive form of you. You're is the contraction form of you are.

15. C
Your vs. you're. Your is the possessive form of you. You're is the contraction form of you are.

16. A
Singular subjects. "The Chinese" is plural, and "a citizen of Bermuda" is singular.

17. A
Sit vs. Set. Set requires an object – something to set down. Sit is something that you do, like sit on the chair.

18. A
Always capitalize proper nouns.

Grammar

19. A
Present progressive "building models" is correct in this sen-

tence.

20. C
Past Perfect tense describes a completed action in the past, before another action in the past.

21. D
The preposition 'to' in this sentence means give.

22. C
"Lie" means to recline, and does not take an object. 'Lay' means to place and does take an object. Peter lay the books on the table, or the telephone poles were lying on the road.

23. B
Cleverest is the proper form to express 'most clever.'

24. B
Past perfect continuous, has been living, is proper because the time element, since 1995, and he is still living there now.

25. B
The correct form is, "please excuse me for being late," or, "please excuse my being late."

English Grammar and Punctuation Tutorials

Capitalization

Although many of the rules for capitalization are pretty straight forward, there are several tricky points that are important to review.

Starting a Sentence

Everyone knows that you need to capitalize the first letter of the first word in a sentence, but is it really all that easy to figure out where one sentence starts and another stops? Take these three examples:

That was the moment it really sunk in: There would be no hockey this year.

It was April and that could mean only one thing: baseball.

We played for hours before heading home; everyone felt tired and happy.

In the first example the first letter after the colon is capitalized while in the second example it is not. That is because everything after the first example's colon is a complete sentence, while after example two's colon there is only one word. In example three you have what could be a complete sentence ("everyone felt tired and happy"), but which is not because it follows a semicolon, making it just another clause instead.

Within a sentence you can have an additional complete sentence if the sentence follows a colon. But if what could be a complete sentence follows a semicolon, it is a clause and does not get capitalized.

Remember that the same rules apply for quotation marks

that apply for colons: A complete sentence inside quotation marks is capitalized, but a single word or phrase is not.

Proper Nouns

The first letter of all proper nouns needs to be capitalized. There are many categories of proper noun. The most common proper nouns are the specific names of people (such as Bill), places (such as Germany) or things (such as Honda Civic). However, there are several less obvious categories of words that should be capitalized as proper nouns.

Historical events such as World War II or the California Gold Rush need to be capitalized.

The names of celestial bodies such as Orion's Belt need to be capitalized.

The names of ethnicities such as African-American or Hispanic need to be capitalized.

Relationship words that replace a person's name such as Mom, Doctor and Mister need to be capitalized. However, this only happens when you use the word to replace the person's name. In the sentence, "My mom went to the store," you do not capitalize it, while in the sentence, "Hey Mom, did you get toothpaste at the store?" you do capitalize it.

Geographical locations are capitalized. This can get a little tricky because capitalized geographical locations and non-capitalized directions are easy to confuse. Saying, "We drove south for hours," is a direction, so the word "south" should not be capitalized. But when saying, "While in the United States, we drove to the South to look at Civil War battlefields," you do capitalize the word "South." The difference is that in the first sentence "south" is just the direction you drove. In the second sentence "the South" is a specific region of the United States that formed itself into the Confederacy during the US Civil War.

Proper Adjectives

Proper adjectives are the adjective forms of proper nouns. People from Germany are German; people from Canada are Canadian. German and Canadian are proper adjectives because they are forms of proper nouns that are used to describe other nouns.

Titles of Works

Titles of works are generally capitalized following a specific pattern. Capitalize all the important words in a sentence. Do not capitalize unimportant words such as prepositions and articles.

For example: Alien Spaceship Spotted over Many of the World's Capitals

Notice that the prepositions "over" and "of," and the article "the" are the only non-capitalized words in the sentence.

Punctuation - Colons, Semicolons, Hyphens, Dashes, Parentheses and Apostrophes

Within a sentence there are several different types of punctuation marks that can denote a pause. Each of these punctuation marks has different rules when it comes to its structure and usage, so we will look at each one in turn.

Colons

The colon is used primarily to introduce information. It can start lists such as in the sentence, "There were several things Susan had to get at the store: bread, cereal, lettuce and tomatoes." Or a colon can be used to point out specific information, such as in the sentence, "It was only then that the group fully realized what had happened: The Martian invasion had begun."

Note that if the information after the colon is a complete sentence, you capitalize and punctuate it exactly like you would a sentence. If, however, it does not constitute a complete sentence, you don't have to capitalize anything. ("Peering out the window Meredith saw them: zombies.")

Semicolons

Semicolons can be thought of as super commas. They denote a stronger stop than a comma does, but they are still weaker than a period, not quite capable of ending a sentence. Semicolons are primarily used to separate independent clauses that are not being separated by a coordinating conjunction. ("Chris went to the store; he bought chips and salsa.") Semicolons can only do this, however, when the ideas in each clause are related. For instance, the sentence, "It's raining outside; my sister went to the movies," is not a proper usage of the semicolon since those clauses have nothing to do with each other.

Semicolons can also be used in lists provided that one or more element in the list is itself made up of a smaller list. If you want to write a list of things you plan to bring to a picnic, and those things only include a Frisbee, a chair and some pasta salad, you would not need to use a semicolon. But if you also wanted to bring plastic knives, forks and spoons, you would need to write your sentence like this: "For our picnic I am bringing a Frisbee; a chair; plastic knives, forks and spoons; and some pasta salad."

Using semicolons like this preserves the smaller list that you have in your larger list.

Hyphens

To join words together to show that they are linked you use hyphens. The most common use of hyphens is to link together words to show that they are working together in a sentence. ("The well-known actor was eating at the table behind us.") This shows explicitly that you are using "well-known" as a single concept and not as two descriptive words in a list.

Hyphens can also be used to split a word in half if you run out of space writing on one line of a page. This is often seen in newspapers and magazines when text is justified to both sides of a page or a column. For example:

The massive earthquake caused surpris-

ingly little damage in the affected areas.

However, you can only use a hyphen in this way if you split the word between syllables. Often students think that they can use hyphens to break up words wherever they want; this is wrong. For the word "surprisingly" you

could have a hyphen between "sur" and "prisingly," "surpris" and "ingly, and between "surprising" and "ly," but nowhere else.

Finally, hyphens can be used to add prefixes to words. This happens a lot in news reports with phrases such as "pro-government troops."

Dashes and Parentheses

Both dashes and parentheses are used to set aside information into parenthetical statements; statements that can be treated as an aside. They do not need to be there for the sentence to make sense, but the information they provide is interesting enough that you feel it should be included. Parentheses are considered stronger than dashes are. (Commas can also be used to separate nonessential information from a sentence, but they are considered to be the weakest of the three.)

As the previous sentence shows, parentheses can surround entire sentences, separating them from the paragraph. Dashes, on the other hand, can separate off the last statement in a sentence. ("Calvin came home and greeted his family for the first time in days—everyone smiled.") Obviously, that last sentence could also be written using a semicolon or as two sentences. The difference is in how you want it to sound to the reader. Should these thoughts be treated as two distinct pieces? Or should everyone smiling at Calvin be part of the main sentence, just separated a bit more strongly—with a slightly longer pause—than a comma could manage?

Apostrophes

There are two primary uses of the apostrophe in English: forming contractions and forming possessive nouns.

Contractions are formed by taking two words and combining them together with an apostrophe replacing the missing letters (do not becomes don't), or by shortening an existing word (cannot becomes can't). Apostrophes can

also make contractions by attaching verbs to nouns or pronouns. ("He's going to the store.")

When making singular nouns possessive the general rule is that you add an 's to the end of singular nouns. (This is Tim's bagel.) When dealing with plural nouns that do not end with the letter –s (such as children), the rule is that you also add an 's to the end of the word. (It was the children's favorite movie.) And when dealing with plural nouns that end with the letter –s, you simply add an apostrophe. (My sisters' favorite game is tag.)

However, and this is an important "however" given the controversy it can cause, when dealing with singular words that end with the letter –s (such as circus), there are two standards for how to make them possessive—each with its own grammar book to back it up.

One standard says that you still add an 's to the end of the word. (This is the circus's biggest tent.) The other says that, since the word ends with an –s, it can only get an apostrophe. (This is the circus' biggest tent.) Some style books, such as the Chicago Manual of Style will go so far as to say that the former option is correct, but to avoid inflaming people's passions on the subject, using the latter is perfectly acceptable. The best thing to do is to find out which style the teacher or editor you are writing for at any given time prefers and conform to it for that person.

Commas

Commas are probably the most commonly used punctuation mark in English. Commas can break the flow of writing to give it a more natural sounding style, and they are the main punctuation mark used to separate ideas. Commas also separate lists, introductory adverbs, introductory prepositional phrases, dates and addresses.

The most rigid way that commas are used is when separating clauses. There are two primary types of clauses in a sentence, independent and subordinate (sometimes called dependent). Independent clauses are clauses that express a complete thought such as, "Tim went to the store." Subordinate clauses, on the other hand, only express partial thoughts that serve to expand upon an independent clause such as, "after the game ended," which you can see is clearly not a complete sentence. (You will learn more about clauses in different lessons.)

The rule for commas with clauses is that a comma must separate the clauses when a subordinate clause comes first in a sentence: "After the game ended, Tim went to the store." But there should not be a comma when a subordinate clause follows an independent clause: "Tim went to the store after the game ended." If you leave the comma out of the first example, you have a run-on sentence. If you add one into the second example, you have a comma-splice error. Also, when you have two independent clauses joined together with a coordinating conjunction, you need to separate them with a comma. "Tim went to the store, and Beth went home."

There are some artistic exceptions to these rules, such as adding a pause for literary effect, but for the most part, they are set in stone.

Commas are also used to separate items in a list. This area of English is unfortunately less clear than it should be, with two separate rules depending on what standard you are following. To understand the two different rules, let's pretend you are having a party at your house, and you are making a list of refreshments your friends will want. You may decide to serve three things: 1) pizza 2) chips 3) drinks. There are two different rules governing how you should punctuate this. According to many grammar books, you would write this as, "At the store I will buy pizza, chips, and drinks." This variation puts a comma after each item in the list. It is the version that the style books used in most college English and history courses will prefer, so it is probably the one you should follow. However, the Associated Press style guide, which is used in college journalism classes and at newspapers and magazines, says the sentence should be written like this: "At the store I will buy pizza, chips and drinks." Here you only use a comma between the first two words, letting the word "and" act as the separator between the last two.

Another important place to use commas is when you have a modifier that describes an element of a sentence, but that does not directly follow the thing it describes. Look at the sentence: "Tim went over to visit Beth, watching the full moon along the way." In this sentence there is no confusion about who is "watching the full moon"; it is Tim, probably as he walks to Beth's house. If you remove the comma, however, you get this: "Tim went over to visit Beth watching the full moon along the way." Now it sounds as though Beth is watching the full moon, and we are forced to wonder what "way" the moon is traveling along.

Commas are also used when adding introductory prepositional phrases and introductory adverbs to sentences. A comma is always needed following an introductory adverb. ("Quickly, Jody ran to the car.") Commas are even necessary when you have an adverb introducing a clause within a sentence, even if the clause not the first clause of the sentence. ("Amanda wanted to go to the movie; however, she knew her homework was more important.")

With introductory prepositional phrases you only add a comma if the phrase (or if a group of introductory phrases) is five or more words long. Thus, the sentence you just read did not have a comma following its introductory prepositional phrase ("With introductory prepositional phrases") because it was only four words. Compare that to this sentence with a five word introductory phrase: "After the ridiculously long class, the friends needed to relax."

The last main way that commas are used in sentences is to separate out information that does not need to be there. For instance, "My cousin Hector, who wore a blue hat at the party, thought you were funny." The fact that Hector wore a blue hat is interesting, but it is not vital to the sentence; it could be removed and not changed the sentence's meaning. For that reason it gets commas around it. Along these lines you should remember that any clause introduced by the word that is considered to provide essential information to the sentence and should not get commas around it. Conversely, any clause starting with the word which is considered nonessential and should not get commas around it.

Quotation Marks

Quotation marks are used in English in a variety of different ways. The most common use of quotation marks is to show quotations either as dialogue or when directly quoting a source in an essay or news article. Fortunately, both of these uses follow the same basic rules.

When you have a quote written as the second part of a sentence, you need to put a comma before the quotation marks and a period inside the quotation marks at the end. (Franklin said, "Let's go to the store.") Conversely, when you have quote as the first part of the sentence with information describing it second, a comma replaces the period at the end of the sentence inside the quotes. ("Let's go to the store," Franklin said.)

If the information in a quote is not a complete sentence you do not need to capitalize it or put commas around it, provided that it is not dialogue. (No one thought the idea of "going to the store" sounded very fun.)

Note that when the last word in a sentence has both a quotation mark and a period attached to it, the period is always inside the quotes. This is the case when you have a complete sentence inside a quote ("Let's go to the store."), and when the last word in a sentence just happens to have quote marks around it (Kerri said I was "mean.") You also need to do the same thing with commas. (Kerri said I was "mean," and it made me feel bad.) However, other punctuation marks such as colons, semicolons and dashes do not follow this rule and should come outside the quotes. (Kerri said I was "mean"; it made me feel bad.)

When you want to use a quote inside a quote, you use the standard double-quotation marks for the outer quote and single-quotation marks for the inner quote. ("The sign on the door said 'no soliciting,' so we went to the next house.")

Quotation marks are also used around certain types of titles. To figure out which ones, it helps to look at which titles are not put in quotes as well.

Titles are generally broken down into two categories: large works and small works. Large works are things such as newspapers, magazines, CDs, books and television shows. The defining characteristic of a large work is that it is able to hold small works in it. Small works are the articles inside newspapers and magazines, the songs on a CD, the chapters in a book and the episodes of a television show. It is small works that get quotation marks around them. (Large works, meanwhile, are either underlined or italicized.)

Using quotation marks correctly in a title looks something like this: The two-page article entitled "San Francisco Giants Win World Series" appeared in yesterday's New York Times. The article title is in quotes, and the newspaper title is in italics.

Common English Usage Mistakes - A Quick Review

Like some parts of English grammar, usage is definitely going to be on the exam and there isn't any tricky strategies or shortcuts to help you get through this section.
Here is a quick review of common usage mistakes.

1. May and Might

'May' can act as a principal verb, which can express permission or possibility.

Examples:

Lets wait, the meeting may have started.
May I begin now?

'May' can act as an auxiliary verb, which an expresses a purpose or wish

Examples:

May you find favour in the sight of your employer.

May your wishes come true.
People go to school so that they may be educated.

The past tense of may is might.

Examples:

I asked if I might begin

'Might' can be used to signify a weak or slim possibility or polite suggestion.

Examples:

You might find him in his office, but I doubt it.
You might offer to help if you want to.

2. Lie and Lay

The verb lay should always take an object. The three forms of the verb lay are: laid, lay and laid.

The verb lie (recline) should not take any object. The three forms of the verb lie are: lay, lie and lain.

Examples:

Lay on the bed.
The tables were laid by the students.
Let the little kid lie.
The patient lay on the table.

The dog has lain there for 30 minutes.

Note: The verb lie can also mean "to tell a falsehood." This verb can appear in three forms: lied, lie, and lied. This is different from the verb lie (recline) mentioned above.

Examples:

The accused is fond of telling lies.
Did she lie?

3. Would and Should

The past tense of shall is 'should', and so "should" generally follows the same principles as "shall."

The past tense of will is "would," and so "would" generally follows the same principles as "will."

The two verbs 'would and should' can be correctly used interchangeably to signify obligation. The two verbs also have some unique uses too. Should is used in three persons to signify obligation.

Examples:

I should go after work.
People should do exercises everyday.
You should be generous.

"Would" is specially used in any of the three persons, to signify willingness, determination and habitual action.

Examples:

They would go for a test run every Saturday.
They would not ignore their duties.
She would try to be punctual.

4. Principle and Auxiliary Verbs

Two principal verbs can be used along with one auxiliary verb as long as the auxiliary verb form suits the two principal verbs.

Examples:

A number of people have been employed and some promoted.

A new tree has been planted and the old has been cut down.

Again note the difference in the verb form.

5. Can and Could

A. Can is used to express capacity or ability.

Examples:

I can complete the assignment today
He can meet up with his target.

B. Can is also used to express permission.

Examples:

Yes, you can begin

In the sentence below, "can" was used to mean the same thing as "may." However, the difference is that the word "can" is used for negative or interrogative sentences, while "may" is used in affirmative sentences to express possibility.

Examples:

They may be correct.   Positive sentence - use may.
Can this statement be correct? A question using "can."
It cannot be correct. Negative sentence using "can."

The past tense of can is could. It can serve as a principal verb when it is used to express its own meaning.

Examples:

In spite of the difficulty of the test, he could still perform well.
"Could" here is used to express ability.

6. Ought

The verb ought should normally be followed by the word to.

Examples:

I *ought to* close shop now.

The verb 'ought' can be used to express:

A. Desirability

You ought to wash your hands before eating.   It is desirable to wash your hands.

B. Probability

She ought to be on her way back by now.   She is probably on her way.

C. Moral obligation or duty

The government ought to protect the oppressed.   It is the government's duty to protect the oppressed.

7. Raise and Rise

Rise
The verb rise means to go up, or to ascend.
The verb rise can appear in three forms, rose, rise, and risen. The verb should not take an object.

Examples:

The bird rose very slowly.
The trees rise above the house.
My aunt has risen in her career.

Raise
The verb raise means to increase, to lift up.
The verb raise can appear in three forms, raised, raise and raised.

Examples:

He raised his hand.
The workers requested a raise.
Do not raise that subject.

8. Past Tense and Past Participle

Pay attention to the proper use these verbs: sing, show, ring, awake, fly, flow, begin, hang and sink.

Mistakes usually occur when using the past participle and past tense of these verbs as they are often mixed up.

Each of these verbs can appear in three forms:

Sing, Sang, Sung.
Show, Showed, Showed/Shown.
Ring, Rang, Rung.
Awake, awoke, awaken
Fly, Flew, Flown.
Flow, Flowed, Flowed.

Begin, Began, Begun.
Hang, Hanged, Hanged (a criminal)
Hang, Hung, Hung (a picture)
Sink, Sank, Sunk.

Examples:

The stranger rang the door bell. (simple past tense)
I have rung the door bell already. (past participle - an action completed in the past)

The stone sank in the river. (simple past tense)
The stone had already sunk. (past participle - an action completed in the past)

The meeting began at 4:00.
The meeting has begun.

9. Shall and Will

When speaking informally, the two can be used interchangeably. In formal writing, they must be used correctly.

"Will" is used in the second or third person, while "shall" is used in the first person. Both verbs are used to express a time or even in the future.

Examples:

I shall, We shall (First Person)
You will (Second Person)
They will (Third Person)

This principle however reverses when the verbs are to be used to express threats, determination, command, willingness, promise or compulsion. In these instances, will is now used in first person and shall in the second and third person.

Examples:

I will be there next week, no matter what.
This is a promise, so the first person "I" takes "will."

You shall ensure that the work is completed.
This is a command, so the second person "you" takes "shall."

I will try to make payments as promised.
This is a promise, so the first person "I" takes "will."

They shall have arrived by the end of the day.
This is a determination, so the third person "they" takes shall.

Note
A. The two verbs, shall and will should not occur twice in the same sentence when the same future is being referred to

Example:

I shall arrive early if my driver is here on time.

B. Will should not be used in the first person when questions are being asked

Examples:

Shall I go ?
Shall we go?

Subject Verb Agreement

Verbs in any sentence must agree with the subject of the sentence both in person and number. Problems usually occur when the verb doesn't correspond with the right subject or the verb fails to match the noun close to it.

Unfortunately, there is no easy way around these principles

- no tricky strategy or easy rule. You just have to memorize them.

Here is a quick review:

The verb to be, present (past)

Person	Singular	Plural
First	I am (was)	we are (were)
Second	you are (were)	you are (were)
Third	he, she, it is (was)	they are (were)

The verb to have, present (past)

Person	Singular	Plural
First	I have (had)	we have (had)
Second	you have (had)	you have (had)
Third	he, she, it has (had)	they have (had)

Regular verbs, e.g. to walk, present (past)

Person	Singular	Plural
First	I walk (walked)	we walk (walked)
Second	you walk (walked)	you walk (walked)
Third	he, she, it walks (walked)	they work (walked)

1. Every and Each

When nouns are qualified by "every" or "each," they take a singular verb even if they are joined by 'and'

Examples:

Each mother and daughter *was* a given separate test.
Every teacher and student *was* properly welcomed.

2. Plural Nouns

Nouns like measles, tongs, trousers, riches, scissors etc. are all plural.

Examples:

The trousers *are* dirty.
My scissors *have* gone missing.
The tongs *are* on the table.

3. With and As Well

Two subjects linked by "with" or "as well" should have a verb that matches the first subject.

Examples:

The pencil, with the papers and equipment, *is* on the desk.
David as well as Louis is coming.

4. Plural Nouns

The following nouns take a singular verb:

> politics, mathematics, innings, news, advice, summons, furniture, information, poetry, machinery, vacation, scenery

Examples:

The machinery *is* difficult to assemble
The furniture *has* been delivered
The scenery *was* beautiful

5. Single Entities

A proper noun in plural form that refers to a single entity requires a singular verb. This is a complicated way of saying; some things appear to be plural, but are really singular, or some nouns refer to a collection of things but the collection is really singular.

Examples:

The United Nations Organization *is* the decision maker in the matter.

Here the "United Nations Organization" is really only one "thing" or noun, but is made up of many "nations."

The book, "The Seven Virgins" *was* not available in the library.

Here there is only one book, although the title of the book is plural.

6. Specific Amounts are always singular

A plural noun that refers to a specific amount or quantity that is considered as a whole (dozen, hundred, score etc) requires a singular verb.

Examples:

60 minutes *is* quite a long time.
Here "60 minutes" is considered a whole, and therefore one

item (singular noun).

The first million is the most difficult.

7. Either, Neither and Each are always singular

The verb is always singular when used with: either, each, neither, every one and many.

Examples:

Either of the boys *is* lying.
Each of the employees *has* been well compensated
Many a police officer *has* been found to be courageous
Every one of the teachers *is* responsible

8. Linking with Either, Or, and Neither match the second subject

Two subjects linked by "either," "or," "nor" or "neither" should have a verb that matches the second subject.

Examples:

Neither David nor Paul *will* be coming.
Either Mary or Tina *is* paying.
Note
If one of the subjects linked by "either," "or," "nor" or "neither" is in plural form, then the verb should also be in plural, and the verb should be close to the plural subject.

Examples:
Neither the mother *nor* her kids *have* eaten.
Either Mary *or* her *friends are* paying.

9. Collective Nouns are Plural

Some collective nouns such as poultry, gentry, cattle, vermin etc. are considered plural and require a plural verb.

Examples:

The *poultry are* sick.
The *cattle are* well fed.

Note
Collective nouns involving people can work with both plural and singular verbs.

Examples:

Nigerians are known to be hard working
Europeans live in Africa

10. Nouns that are Singular and Plural

Nouns like deer, sheep, swine, salmon etc. can be singular or plural and require the same verb form.

Examples:

The swine is feeding. (singular)
The swine are feeding. (plural)

The salmon is on the table. (singular)
The salmon are running upstream. (plural)

11. Collective Nouns are Singular

Collective nouns such as Army, Jury, Assembly, Committee, Team etc should carry a singular verb when they subscribe to one idea. If the ideas or views are more than one, then the verb used should be plural.

Examples:

The committee is in agreement in their decision.

The committee were in disagreement in their decision.
The jury has agreed on a verdict.
The jury were unable to agree on a verdict.

12. Subjects links by "and" are plural.

Two subjects linked by "and" always require a plural verb

Examples:

David and John are students.

Note
If the subjects linked by "and" are used as one phrase, or constitute one idea, then the verb must be singular

The color of his socks and shoe is black.
Here "socks and shoe" are two nouns, however the subject is "color" which is singular.

Writing Self-Assessment Part II
Essay Revision

Alvin Lee's Guitar

Only a few of his contemporaries rocked the rock n' roll era with their guitars like Alvin Lee.[1] Even at the age of 67, just a year before his demise, he produced the finest album of his five-decade long career with *Still on the Road to Freedom*.[2] Strikingly flamboyant with his guitar, Lee gained millions of admirers around the world with hits like "*I'd Love to Change the World*," "*On the Road to Freedom*" and "*Freedom for the Stallion*" which <u>reflected and showed the popular worldviews people had at the time</u> of their release.[3]

Alvin Lee began playing guitar at an early age, and was influenced by his parents' passion for music and inspired by the likes of Chuck Berry and Scotty Moore.[4] Lee started his career as the lead vocalist and guitarist in a band named the Jaybirds at the famous Marquee Club in London in 1962.[5] A few years later the band changed its name to *Ten Years After* and released its debut album under the new name.[6] Lee's lightning fast guitar playing at the Woodstock Festival gained him instant stardom and Lee was asked to tour the US.[7]

In the coming years, he worked with rock legends like Mylon LeFevre, George Harrison, Steve Winwood, Ronnie Wood and Mick Fleetwood and released the country rock masterpiece *On the Road to Freedom* which brought him overwhelming trans-Atlantic popularity.[8] In subsequent years, he continued addressing social and global issues in albums like *A Space in Time*, *Pump Iron!*, *Let It Rock* and *Rocket Fuel*.[9] With many of his songs, such as, "*I'd Love to Change the World*," Lee used the power of rock music to show his solidarity with ordinary people and their worldviews.[10] He also went on with inspiring the upcoming generations of rock stars by producing expressive and tasteful guitar performances in his 1980s albums *Free Fall*, *RX5* and *Detroit Diesel*.[11]

1. **What is the main idea of the first paragraph?**

    a. Alvin Lee's achievements

    b. Alvin Lee's inspiration

    c. The Rock n' Roll era

    d. Alvin Lee's guitar playing skill

2. **Which of the following changes is/are needed in sentence 6?**

    a. A few years later, the band changed its name to *Ten Years After* and released its debut album under the new name.

    b. A few years later, the band changed its name to *Ten Years After*, and released its debut album under the new name.

    c. A few years later the band changed its name to *Ten Years After*, and released its debut album under the new name.

    d. A few years later, the band changed its name to *Ten Years After* and, released its debut album under the new name.

3. **Which of the following would best replace the underlined portion of sentence 3?**

    a. reflected and showed the popular worldviews people have at the time of their release

    b. reflected the popular worldviews at the time of their release

    c. reflected and showed the popular worldviews people have at the time of their release

    d. No changes necessary.

4. Which of the following changes are needed to sentence 11?

> a. He also went on inspiring the upcoming generations of rock stars by producing expressive and tasteful guitar performances in his 1980s albums *Free Fall*, *RX5* and *Detroit Diesel*.
>
> b. He also went on to inspire the upcoming generations of rock stars by producing expressive and tasteful guitar performances in his 1980s albums *Free Fall*, *RX5* and *Detroit Diesel*.
>
> c. He also went with inspiring the upcoming generations of rock stars by producing expressive and tasteful guitar performances in his 1980s albums *Free Fall*, *RX5* and *Detroit Diesel*. .
>
> d. He also went on to inspiring the upcoming generations of rock stars by producing expressive and tasteful guitar performances in his 1980s albums *Free Fall*, *RX5* and *Detroit Diesel*. .

A Personal Satellite?

Many of us are already so loaded with technology, we don't have time to think about integrating even more! [1] In fact at this point it seems impossible to think about personal satellites now, just as we once thought about smart phones. [2] The reality of personal spacecraft is still in the realm and area of Star Trek and geeky space fantasies. [3]

However, the days when each of us will has our own personal satellite are not far away! [4] And what is even more exciting is they will be available for the cost of an iPhone! [5] At least, according to Zach Manchester, the inventor of the nano-satellite KickSat.[6] "I'd like to think of it as the people's satellite," says Manchester. [7] "We're pushing towards a personal satellite, where you can afford to put your own thing in space." [8]

The KickSat, a 30 cm. long hardware pack, is a space enthusiast's dream. [9] It contains the basics of a fully functional satellite. [10] Inside its compact design, the KickSat itself contains 200 more tinier satellites of cubic shape called "Sprites." [11] The Sprites are engineered and programmed so that they can be tracked and communicate via radio signals with a ground station on earth. [12] Each Sprite is available for purchase and is uniquely named after the sponsors who support Zach's project. [13] Anyone who has sponsored a Sprite will be able to track their personal satellite from a ground station installed in their balcony or roof! [14]

5. What is the best way to re-write the underlined portion of sentence 3?

    a. the realm of

    b. the realms of

    c. the realms and areas of

    d. no changes are necessary

6. What is the best way to re-write the underlined portion of sentence 4?

    a. the days when each of us will have her own

    b. the days when each of us will have our own

    c. the days when each of us will have their own

    a. d. no changes are necessary

7. Which of the following changes are needed to sentence 2?

a. In fact at this point it seems impossible to think about personal satellites now - just as we once thought about smart phones.

b. In fact, at this point, it seems impossible to think about personal satellites now, just as we once thought about smart phones.

c. In fact, at this point, it seems impossible to think about personal satellites now - just as we once thought about smart phones.

d. In fact at this point, it seems impossible to think about personal satellites now, just as we once thought about smart phones.

8. Which of the following changes are needed to sentence 11?

a. Under its compact design, the KickSat itself contains 200 more tiny satellites of cubic shape called "Sprites."

b. Under its compact design, the KickSat itself contains 200 more tiny satellites of cubic shapes called "Sprites."

c. Inside its compact design, the KickSat itself contains 200 tinier satellites of cubic shapes called "Sprites."

d. With its compact design, the KickSat contains 200 tiny cube-shaped satellites called "Sprites."

Baseball in Uganda

They were denied participation the year earlier, but the Ugandan kids made their mark at the 2012 Little League World Series. [1] The Lugazi Little League team members were the darlings of the world baseball stage when they participated in their dream tournament. [2] This time, they made sure all their participants were age-qualified; all the new stars were 11 years old. [3] No, not really forged to any extent. [4] And what is more interesting, they are all native Ugandans; a fact that points to the huge baseball talent in Uganda. [5]

Baseball talent isn't appreciated in the East African country dominated by soccer athletes, however. [6] And that is what has captured the attention of the sponsors interested in investing on the emerging generation of players. [7] After their disappointing disqualification for alleged forging of documents in 2011, many investors had already offered financial commitments to develop the sport in the country. [8] Proposals for infrastructure development had already been made and organizers were looking to boost government support for the new sport. [9]

The Uganda Baseball and Softball Association has started construction of its first ever home diamond thanks to funding by the government of Japan. [10] Apart from that, some organizations and professional players are helping the Lugazi Little League with equipment, coaching, support staff organization of events and so on. [11] Many NGOs are offering academic scholarships to native Ugandans who wish to pursue their higher studies and become a baseball professional in the USA. [12]

After their remarkable appearance in the 2012 event, youngsters in Uganda are turning their attention to this new game. [13] With the new season of the World Series only a few months away, we will soon witness if young Ugandans are really interested in the sport. [14]

9. Which of the following changes to sentence 11 would focus attention on the main idea of the third paragraph?

a. Apart from that, some organizations and professional players are organizing charity matches for raising funds for helping the sport develop in the country.

b. Apart from that, some non-profit organizations are donating money to improve the infrastructure of the country by building roads and highways to promote the sport.

c. Apart from that, the Lugazi League has been receiving substantial funding from non-governmental organizations and fellow baseball pros who provide assistance with equipment, coaching, support staff and organization of events.

d. Apart from that, some professional players are promoting the Lugazi Little League by participating in them directly or indirectly.

10. Which of the following changes are needed to sentence 7?

a. And that is what has attracted the attention of the sponsors interested in investing on the emerging generation of players.

b. And that is what has attracted the attention of the sponsors to invest in the emerging generation of players.

c. And that is what has captured the attention of the sponsors for investing on the emerging generation of players.

d. And that is what has attracted the attention of the sponsors who are interested in investing on the emerging generation of players.

Answer Key

1. A
The main idea of the first paragraph is Alvin Lee's achievements.

2. A
The edited version of sentence 6 is, "A few years later, the band changed its name to Ten Years After and released its debut album under the new name."

Choice A places a comma after the prepositional phrase "A few years later" that expresses time. No other punctuation is necessary for a coordinate conjunction "and" as proposed by choices B and C since the clause "released its debut album under the new name" is a subordinate rather than an independent one. Choice D offers an incorrect suggestion, placing a comma after "and."

3. B
Original
"... which reflected and showed the popular worldviews people had at the time of their release."

Edited
"... reflected the popular worldviews at the time of their release."

This is a much shorter and more concise sentence. "Reflected and showed" is redundant, and "worldviews people had at the time" is wordy.

4. B
Suggested changes to sentence 11 are, "He also went on to inspire upcoming generations of rock stars by producing expressive and tasteful guitar performances in his 1980s albums. *Free Fall*, *RX5* and *Detroit Diesel*."

The correction offered in choice B is the only appropriate one since the gerund form of "inspire" is not appropriate when starting the action. In this case, the author expresses initiation of the process of inspiring more than one generation. So, rather than continuing an already started process, this sentence refers to beginning of an additional process of inspiring as indicated by "also." The gerund form is used rather when the action represented by the verb is in a continuous process already in motion. Therefore, the to-infinitive must be used. As a result choice A can be eliminated. Choices C and D offer no valid gerund or infinitive.

5. A
The underlined phrase, "the realm and area of" is redundant and wordy. This can be replaced with, "the realm of."

6. B
The subject, "each of us" must agree with the verb, "have" so the correct phrase is, "the days when each of us will have our own"

7. C
The revised version of sentence 2 is, "In fact, at this point, it seems impossible to think about personal satellites now - just as we once thought about smart phones."

This choice uses the correct punctuation; two commas, one before and one after the subordinate conjunction "at this point," which bridges the adverbial clause after it with the adjective at the start of the sentence. Also the use of a hyphen to express extended thought is correct in choice C.

8. D
The only choice with correct grammar is choice D. It replaces "more tiny" with "tiny" as well as "cubic shaped" with "cube-shaped." Tinier is the correct comparative form of "tiny" and "cubic" is the adjective that must describe the singular noun "shape," not "shapes" or any of its verbal forms. Two word adjectives, such as "a 3-mile race" are hyphenated.

"Under its compact design" is incorrect. Replace with, "with its compact design ... "

9. C
The changes to sentence 11 are, "Apart from that, the Lugazi League has been receiving substantial funding from non-governmental organizations and fellow baseball pros who provide assistance with equipment, coaching, support staff

and organization of events."

When the sentence is updated to this form, it remains consistent with the factual information provided in the original sentence, and at the same time, reflects best the main idea of the paragraph. Choices A and B do not have any factual basis as compared to choice C and can be eliminated. Choice D does not have any factual basis either and it is irrelevant to the main idea of the paragraph as it talks about promoting the sport rather than funding it.
Generally, avoid using "and so on."

10. B
Changes to sentence 7 are, "And that is what has attracted the attention of the sponsors to invest in the emerging generation of players."

Choice B offers the correct English usage as well as grammar. The synonym "attract" is more appropriate and also omission of a redundant "interested in" along with "the attention of sponsors" is correctly suggested. In addition, to-infinitive form of "invest" is used rather than the gerund in the original form. Choice A contains the redundant expression "interested in" and so is inappropriate. Choice C still has the synonym "capture" and the gerund noun form "investing" is disputable. Choice D once again has the redundant expression as in choice A.

How to Write an Essay

Writing an essay can be a difficult process, especially if you are under time constraints such as during an exam. Here are three simple steps to help you to write a solid, well thought out essay:

1. **Brainstorm** potential themes and general ideas for your essay.
2. **Outline** your essay step by step, including subheadings for ease of understanding.
3. **Write** your essay carefully being aware of proper grammar and sentence structure.

Brainstorming

You should first spend some time thinking about the general subject of the essay. If the essay is asking a question, you must make sure to answer this fully in your essay. You may find it helpful to highlight key words in your assignment or use a simple spider diagram to jot down key ideas.

Example

> Read the following information and complete the following assignment:
>
> Joseph Conrad is a Polish author who lived in England for most of his life and wrote a prolific amount of English literature. Much of his work was completed during the height of the British Empire's colonial imperialism.
>
> Assignment: What impact has Joseph Conrad had on modern society? Present your point of view on the matter and support it with evidence. Your evidence may include

reasoning, logic, examples from readings, your own experience, and observations.

Joseph Conrad

Background? sailor, adventure, Polish immigrant, Youth, Nostromo, Heart of Darkness
Themes in his works? ivory, silver trading, colonialism, corruption, greed
Thoughts? descent into madness, nature of evil

Outlining (or planning)

An outline or plan is critical to organize your thoughts and ideas fully and logically. There are many ways to do this; the easiest is to write down the following headings:

1. Title
2. Introduction
3. Body
4. Conclusion

You should then jot down key ideas and themes that fit logically under the appropriate heading. This plan is now the backbone of your essay.

Tip: Even if you are not required to produce an outline or plan for the assignment, you should always leave it with your essay in the exam booklet or the back of the assignment paper. Simply draw a line across it and write 'plan' or 'outline'. This demonstrates to the reader the approach you use in formulating and finally writing your essay.

Writing the essay

Your introduction is what will help the reader to decide whether they want to read the rest of your essay. The introduction also introduces the subject matter and allows you to provide a general background to the reader. The first sentence is very important and you should avoid starting the essay with openers such as 'I will be comparing...'

Example

> Born as Józef Teodor Konrad Korzeniowski on December 3rd, 1857, Joseph Conrad led an adventurous life. As a Polish immigrant, Conrad never quite fit into England where he spent most of his adult life. As a younger man, Conrad made a living off sailing voyages. These swashbuckling experiences soon had him writing tales of the high seas such as one of his first works, Youth. While his early, adventurous work was of high quality, Conrad is best remembered for shedding light on the exploitative side of colonialism. Age and experience led him to start writing about (and challenging) the darker side of the imperial way of thinking. Conrad's work has forever soured words such as colonialism and imperialism.

In the main part, or body of your essay, you should always be yourself and be original.

- Avoid using clichés.
- Be aware of your tone.
- Consider the language that you use. Avoid jargon and slang. Use clear prose and imagery.
- Your writing should always flow; remember to use transitions, especially between paragraphs. Read aloud in your head to make sure a paragraph sounds right.
- Always try to use a new paragraph for new ideas.

Example

> *Conrad's written fiction focused on themes such as greed and power. He portrayed these two concepts as purveyors of evil. Greed and power may take on different guises, but the end result would always be the same.*
>
> *Perhaps his most famous piece, The Heart of Darkness, is about the descent of an English*

> ivory trader, Mr. Kurtz, into madness. We are taken up a river resembling the Congo by a narrator, Marlow, who is sent to retrieve Mr. Kurtz. Marlow eventually finds that Kurtz has been diluted by power and greed, the two things that spurred on colonialism in Africa. Kurtz has taken charge of a large tribe of natives (that he brutalizes) and has been hoarding ivory for himself.
>
> Much of Conrad's later work was cut from the same vein as The Heart of Darkness. His crowning achievement is considered Nostromo where he takes an idealistic hero and corrupts him with colonial greed. Only this time the greed is for silver, not ivory.
>
> Conrad's work resonates with readers partly because it was semi-autobiographical. Where his experience sailing the high seas helped bring his adventure stories to light, likewise did his experience witnessing atrocities in Africa reverberate through his writing.

The conclusion is your last chance to impress your reader and brings your entire essay to a logical close. You may want to link your conclusion back to your introduction or provide some closing statements. Do not panic if you cannot close your essay off completely. Few subjects offer closure.

Your conclusion should always be consistent with the rest of the essay and you should never introduce a new idea in your conclusion. It is also important to remember that a weak conclusion can diminish the impact of a good essay.

Example

> In sum, Joseph Conrad's life experiences and masterful writing left a lasting impact on the image of progress and what it meant to "move forward." He brought to light the cost in human lives that was required for Europe to continue

mining natural resources from foreign lands. Joseph Conrad had a permanent impact on imperial culture, and colonial brutality has been on the decline ever since his work was published.

Presentation

Poor grammar and punctuation can ruin an otherwise good essay. You should always follow any requirements about the presentation of your essay, such as word count. You should also make sure that your writing is legible. Always allow time for one final read-through before submission.

Tip: If you are able to, write with double spacing. If you make a mistake, you can cross it out and write the correction on the blank line above.

Some final points to think about for writing a solid, well thought out essay:

- A good essay will contain a strong focus.

- There is no set essay structure but you can use sub-headings for better readability.

- Avoid particularly sensitive or controversial material. If you must write about something controversial, always make sure to include counter arguments.

- Your essay may have little to do with the subject itself; it is about what you make of the subject.

- Your essay can include examples from your readings, experience, studies or observations.

- Spend time doing practice essays and looking at sample essays beforehand.

Another Example

Lets look at another example using the three steps required to write a good essay:

1. **Brainstorming**
2. **Outlining**
3. **Writing**

Using a second essay, we can now explore these three steps in further detail.

Brainstorming

Example

> *Think about the information that follows and the assignment below.*
>
> *People often quote the last two lines of Robert Frost's "The Road not Taken" as being metaphorical for success. The line's read "I took the one less travelled by, / And that has made all the difference" (19, 20).*
>
> *Assignment: Analyze and interpret this poem. Consider the poem's place in Modernist culture and Robert Frost's personal experiences. Read in between the lines and identify the more complex aspects/themes of this poem. Outline and complete an essay that challenges the point of view presented above, that the poem is synonymous with success. Provide evidence backed up by logic, experience, research, and/or examples from the poem.*

The assignment and key words that appear in the brief above are being highlighted. This confirms that the essay is not asking a specific question, but rather it is asking for discussion of the subject matter and phrases.
This is the time to take a few moments to jot down initial

thoughts about the assignment. Do not worry too much about proper grammar at this point, just get all your thoughts down on paper:

"The Road Not Taken" by Robert Frost

> **Background?** Modernist poetry
> **Themes?** Life decisions, regret, fate, the unknown future
> **Thoughts?** The diverging roads are symbolic, the sigh at end signifies regret, life has many twists and turns, you can end up in a drastically different situation later after a simple decision now

Outlining (or Planning)

Outlining or planning is the next important stage in the process and you should always spend a few minutes writing a plan. This plan is just as important as the essay itself. You can also note how much **time** you may want to spend on a particular section. Make sure to assign headings to each main section of the essay and include important questions/themes you want to address.

Example

> **1. Title**
>
> **2. Essay introduction**
> *Identify and discuss the underlying theme/s in Robert Frost's "The Road Not Taken"*
> *What was Frost's background and its applicability to understanding this poem?*
>
> **3. Essay body**
> *Quick summary of the poem*
> *Discuss key themes and other concepts*
> *Discuss how these things relate to Modernism*
>
> **4. Essay conclusion**
> *Rephrase the themes of Robert Frost's poem and their place in modernist doctrine*

This plan is now the outline for the essay.

Writing the Essay

The introduction is important, as it needs to introduce the reader to the essay in a way that will encourage them to continue reading. A good introduction will introduce the subject matter to a reader and point out relevant information that may be helpful to know when reading the rest of the essay.

Example

> Identify and discuss the underlying theme/s in Robert Frost's "The Road Not Taken"
>
> *Robert Frost wrote during the artistic movement after World War I known as Modernism. One purpose of modernism was to remake things in a new light, to analyze and change symptoms of societies that had plunged the European world into a grisly war. Frost's poem, "The Road Not Taken," carries with it a burden of regret that was a staple of Modernist art.*

This introduction opens with what explaining about the time period of Robert Frost and real life influences to the theme of his poem, "The Road Not Taken." It contains some powerful language that will encourage the reader to continue reading and gives a solid base in understanding the remainder of the essay.

The main part or **body of the essay** is also very important:

Example

> *"The Road Not Taken" was almost assuredly influenced by Robert Frost's personal life. He was very familiar with facing difficult decisions. Frost had to make the decision to send both his sister and daughter to mental institutions. His son Carol committed suicide at the age of 38. The list of loss Frost experienced in his life goes on, but it suffices to say he was familiar with questioning the past.*

With no other hints of the narrator's identity, it is best to assume that he is a man similar to Frost himself. The poem itself is about a nameless narrator reflecting on when he travelled through the autumn woods one day. He had come across a split in the road and expresses regret that he could not travel both. Each road is described as looking similar and as having equal wear but it is also mentioned one was grassier. The roads were unknown to the narrator, and also shared equal possibilities in how well they may or may not be around their bends. He tells his listener with a sigh that he had made his decision and had taken "the road less travelled by" (19). Even though he had little idea which road would be better in the long run, the one he chose proved difficult.

This poem is a collection of all the insecurities and possibilities that come with even the simplest decisions. We experience the sorrow expressed by the narrator in the opening lines with every decision we make. For all the choices you make in life, there is a counterweight of choices you have not made. In a way, we are all missing out on half of our lives' possibilities. This realization causes a mixture of regret and nostalgia, but also stokes in us the keen awareness that missed opportunities are inevitable and regretting them is a waste of energy. We often find ourselves stuck, as the narrator is, between questioning the decisions we've made and knowing that this natural process isn't exactly productive.

Unsolvable regret and nostalgia are things that the Modernists fought with on a regular basis. They often experimented in taking happenings of the past and reinventing them to fit a new future.

The body of the essay opens with providing a brief overview of Robert Frost's personal life and his life's relevance to the over arching theme of dealing with difficult decisions in the poem, "The Road Not Taken."

A new paragraph starts where appropriate and at the end of the discussion of Robert Frost's life, a **transition** moves the reader back to the start of the book (closing off this section). This also helps to move the reader towards the next discussion point.

The tone of this essay is formal, mainly because of the seriousness of the subject – regret and nostalgia plays a major role in people's lives all around the world.

For the conclusion, there will be a summary of the main discussion. While it is ideal for you to impress the reader with your writing, more importantly you need to make sure you cover all your bases and address the assignment appropriately with a closing statement about any important points you discussed in the body of your essay.

Example

> *In conclusion, Robert Frost's poem "The Road Not Taken" deals with themes of fate, regret, sorrow, and the many possibilities our decisions hold. Consider how easy it would be to upturn your life today if you made a few decisions you normally wouldn't. Frost's poem forces us to consider the twists and turns our lives take. Perhaps with a sigh, we could all think about the choices that for us have made all the difference.*

This conclusion is consistent with the rest of the essay in terms of style. There are no new ideas introduced and it has referred to the main points in the assignment title.

Finally, a full read-through is necessary before submission. It only takes a couple of minutes to read through and pick up any errors. Remember to double space to leave room for any corrections to be made. You can also leave spacing at the end of each paragraph in case you should need to add an additional sentence or two.

Formulating A Thesis

Formulating a thesis statement can be one of the most challenging and frustrating things when writing an essay. However, it is also one of the most important things. A thesis statement summarizes your entire essay or argument into one sentence. A good thesis statement is unbiased, limited to one main idea, and has no doubts. Does it sound complicated? Well, let's un-complicate it! The best way to learn about a good thesis is to compare and contrast some bad ones.

Let's start with some informative thesis statements. Informative thesis statements don't have an opinion so they are typically easier to write. To begin with, let's look at a familiar movie.

-Aladdin is sort of a criminal, but I think he's really nice, and he falls in love with the princess and they defeat Jafar and live happily ever after.

-Aladdin is a lovable thief who falls in love with a princess and uses his wit and good heart to save a kingdom from the evil sorcerer, Jafar.

Both of these statements summarize the movie Aladdin. However, which one of these is a better thesis statement? The second one. Why? Well, let's look closer. The first statement gives a quick summary of the movie, but look at the language. That statement uses phrases like "sort of" and "I think." These don't make very good thesis statements because of their uncertainty and bias. The second statement, though, is very confident and provides just enough information to the reader. There is no room for doubt and it is quick and to the point. These are qualities of a solid thesis statement.

While the example above was simply an informative thesis, most thesis statements make a claim or argument. Let's take a look at another example that declares an opinion.

-I feel that Harry Potter is one of the greatest characters ever written because I believe he persevered and was very strong through the gravest of evils.

-Harry Potter is one of the greatest characters ever written because he consistently shows strength and perseverance through the gravest of evils.

These thesis statements are very similar. However, the second one is still better. Let's look at why. Take a look at some of the language in the first thesis statement. Are there doubts? Are there biased statements? "I feel" and "I believe" are both biased phrases. The second statement removes the biased statements and becomes a much stronger thesis.

Here are a few more tips that might help:

- **A thesis statement is always a declarative statement and never a question.**

    Bad: Is Harry Potter the greatest character ever written because of his strength and perseverance through the gravest of evils?

- **A good thesis statement never uses "qualifiers" like might, maybe, perhaps, most likely, possibly, etc.**

    Bad: Harry Potter might be the greatest character ever written because he possibly shows the most strength and perseverance through what is most likely the gravest of evils in literature.

- **Thesis statements don't argue both sides of a debate.**

    Bad: Harry Potter is the greatest character ever written because of his strength and perseverance through the gravest of evils, but Hermione is also the greatest character because she is incredibly smart and helps Harry defeat Voldemort.

Let's look at two more examples to clarify this even more. Look at the essay prompts and then look at the two thesis examples that follow. Determine which thesis statement is better.

Does participation in extracurricular activities in high school help students perform better academically?

> -High school students who are involved in extracurricular activities are more engaged in school which leads to better academic performances.

> -High school students who are involved in extracurricular activities are usually more engaged in school which can lead to better academic performances usually.

Number 1 is better. It leaves out all the extra biased and uncertain language and makes a clear and concise argument. Let's try one more.

Should all high school teachers be required to have master's degrees before teaching?

> -High school teachers educate the future generation and should be required to have a master's degree so they are experts in teaching their subjects, even though I know many teachers who do not have master's degrees who are great at their job.

> -High school teachers educate the future generation and should be required to have a master's degree so they are experts in teaching their subjects.

The second thesis statement is better here. What is wrong with the first one? It brings in personal information by using "I" and it also argues both sides of the debate. The second is concise and states a clear opinion without any personal bias.

Writing good thesis statements takes practice so don't get discouraged if you write two or three before you find the right one for your essay! You may also need to write a few sentences that summarize your main idea and opinion before you tackle the full thesis statement. This is okay! Find what works for you! Just remember the main ideas. Your thesis should be clear and concise, it should state your opinion without any doubts, and it should be unbiased.

Common Essay Mistakes - Example 1

Whether the topic is love or action, reality television shows damage society. Viewers witness the personal struggles of strangers and they experience an outpouring of emotions in the name of entertainment. This can be dangerous on many levels. Viewers become numb to real emotions and values. Run the risk of not interpreting a dangerous situation correctly. 1 The reality show participant is also at risk because they are completely exposed. 2 The damage to both viewers and participants leads to the destruction of our healthy societal values.

Romance reality shows are dangerous to the participants and contribute to the emotional problems witnessed in society today as we set up a system built on equality and respect, shows like "The Bachelor" tear it down. 3 In front of millions of viewers every week, young women compete for a man. Twenty-five women claim to be in love with a man they just met. The man is reduced to an object they compete for. There are tears, fights, and manipulation aimed at winning the prize. 4 Imagine a young woman's reality when she returns home and faces the scrutiny of viewers who watched her unravel on television every Monday night. These women objectify themselves and have learned 5 that relationships are a combination of hysteria and competition. This does not give hope to a society based on family values and equality.

6 While incorporating the same manipulations and breakdown of relationships offered on "The Bachelor," shows like "Survivor" add another level of danger. Not only are they building a society based on lying to each other, they are competing in physical challenges that become dangerous. In the name of entertainment, these challenges become increasingly physical and are usually held in a hostile environment. The viewer's ability to determine the safety of an activity is messed up. 7 To entertain and preserve their pride, participants continue in competitions regardless of the danger level. For example, 8 participants on "Survivor" have sustained serious injuries as heart attack and burns.

Societal rules are based on the safety of its citizens, not on hurting yourself for entertainment.

Reality shows of all kinds are dangerous to participants. They damage society. 9

1. Correct sentence fragments. Who/what runs the risk? Add a subject or combine sentences. Try: "Viewers become numb to real emotions and run the risk of not interpreting a dangerous situation correctly."

2. Correct redundant phrases. Try: "The reality show participant is also at risk because they are exposed."

3. Correct run-on sentences. Decide which thoughts should be separated. Try: "Romance reality shows are dangerous to participants and contribute to the emotional problems of society today. As we support a system built on equality and respect, shows like "The Bachelor" tear it down."

4. Vary sentence structure and length. Try: "Twenty-five women claim to be in love with a man who is reduced to being the object of competition. There are tears, fights, and manipulation aimed at winning the prize."

5. Use active voice. Try: These women objectify themselves and learned that relationships are a combination of hysteria and competition.

6. Use transitions to tie paragraphs together. Try: Start the paragraph with, "Action oriented reality shows are equally as dangerous to the participants."

7. Avoid casual language/slang. Try: "The viewer's ability to determine the safety of an activity is compromised."

8. Don't address the essay. Avoid phrases like "for example" and "in conclusion." Try: "Participants on "Survivor" have sustained serious injuries in the form of heart attack and burns.

9. Leave yourself time to write a strong conclusion! Try: Designate 3-5 minutes for writing your conclusion.

Common Essay Mistakes - Example 2

Questioning authority makes society stronger. In every aspect our society, there is an authoritative person or group making rules. There is also the group underneath them who are meant to follow. 1 This is true of our country's public schools as well as our federal government. The right to question authority at both of these levels is guaranteed by the United States Declaration of Independence. People are given the ability to question so that authority figures are kept in check 2 and will be forced to listen to the opinions of other people. Questioning authority leads to positive changes in society and preserves what is already working well.

If students never question the authority of a principal's decisions, the best interest of the student body is lost. Good things 3 may not remain in place for the students and no amendment to the rules are sought. Change requires that authority be questioned. An example of this is Silver Head Middle School in Davie, Florida. Last year, the principal felt strongly about enforcing the school's uniform policy. Some students were not bothered by this. 4 Many students felt the policy disregarded their civil rights. A petition voicing student dissatisfaction was signed and presented to the principal. He met with a student representative to discuss the petition. Compromise was reached as a monthly "casual day." The students were able to promote change and peace by questioning authority.

Even at the level of federal government, our country's ultimate authority, the ability to question is the key to the harmony keeping society strong. Most government officials are elected by the public so they have the right to question their authority. 5 If there's a mandate, law, or statement that citizens aren't 6 happy with, they have recourse. Campaigning for or against a political platform and participating in the electoral process give a voice to every opinion. I think elections are very important. 7 Without this questioning and examination of society's laws, the government will represent only the voice of the authority figure. The success of our society is based on the questioning of authority. 8

Society is strengthened by those who question authority. Dialogue is created between people with different visions and change becomes possible. At both the level of public school and of federal government, the positive effects of questioning authority can be witnessed. Whether questioning the decisions of a single principal or the motives of the federal government, it is the willingness of people to question and create change that allows society to grow. A strong society is inspired by many voices, all at different levels. 9 These voices keep society strong.

1. Write concisely. Combine the sentences to improve understanding and cut unnecessary words. Try: "In every aspect of society, there is an authority making rules and a group of people meant to follow them."

2. Avoid slang. Re-word "kept in check." Try: "People are given the ability to question so that authority figures are held accountable and will be forced to listen to the opinions of other people.

2-2. Cut unnecessary words. Try: "People are given the ability to question so that authority figures are held accountable and will listen to other opinions."

3. Use precise language. What are "good things?"Try: "Interesting activities may not remain in place for the students and no amendment to the rules are sought."

Use correct subject-verb agreement. Be careful to identify the correct subject of your sentence. Try: "Interesting activities may not remain in place for the students and no amendment to the rules is sought."

4. Don't add information that doesn't add value to your argument. Cut: "Some students weren't bothered by this."

5. Check for parallel structure. Who has the right to question whose authority? Try: "Having voted them in, the people have the authority to question public officials."

6. Don't use contractions in academic essays. Try: "If there is a mandate, law, or statement that citizens are not happy with, they have recourse."

7. Don't use the pronoun "I" in persuasive essays. Cut opinions. Cut: "I think elections are very important."

8. Use specific examples to prove your argument. Try: Discuss a particular election in depth.

9. Cut redundant sentences. Cut: "A strong society is inspired by many voices, all at different levels."

Writing Concisely

Concise writing is direct and descriptive. The reader follows the writer's thoughts easily. If your writing is concise, a four paragraph essay is acceptable for standardized tests. It's better to write clearly about fewer ideas than to write poorly about many.

This doesn't always mean using fewer words. It means that every word you use is important to the message. Unnecessary or repetitive information dilutes ideas and weakens your writing. The meaning of the word concise comes from the Latin, "to cut up." If it isn't necessary information, don't waste precious testing minutes writing it down.

Being redundant is a quick way to lengthen a sentence or paragraph, but it takes away your power during a timed essay. While many writers use repetition of phrases and key words to make their point, it's important to remove words that don't add value. Redundancy can confuse and lead you away from your subject when you need to write quickly. Be aware that many redundant phrases are part of our daily language and need to be cut from your essay.

For example, "bouquet of flowers" is a redundant phrase as only the word "bouquet" is necessary. Its definition includes flowers. Be especially careful with words you use to stress a point, such as "completely," "totally," and "very."

First of all, I'd like to thank my family.
Revised: First, I'd like to thank my family.

The school *introduced a new* rule.
Revised: The school introduced a rule.

I am *completely full.*
Revised: I am full.

Your glass is *totally empty*!
Revised: Your glass is empty!

Her artwork is *very unique.*
Revised: Her artwork is unique.

Other ways to cut bulk and time include avoiding phrases that have no meaning or power in your essay. Phrases like "in my opinion," "as a matter of fact," and "due to the fact that" are space and time wasters. Also, change passive verbs to active voice.

In my opinion, the paper is well written.
Revised: The paper is well written.

The book *was written* by the best students.
Revised: The best students wrote the book.

The teacher *is listening* to the students.
The teacher listens to the students.

This assigns action to the subject, shortens, and clarifies the sentence. When time is working against you, precise language is on your side.

Not only should you remove redundant phrases, whole sentences without value should be cut too. Replacing general nouns with specific ones is an effective way to accomplish this.

She screamed as the thing came closer. It was a sharp-toothed dog.
Revised: She screamed as the sharp-toothed dog came closer.

The revised sentence is precise and the paragraph is improved by combining sentences and varying sentence structure. When editing, ask yourself which thoughts should be connected and which need to be separated. Skim each paragraph as you finish writing it and cut as you go.

Leave three to four minutes for final editing. While reading, make a point to pause at every period. This allows you to "hear" sentences the way your reader will, not how you meant them to sound. This will help you find the phrases and sentences that need to be cut or combined. The result is an essay a grader will appreciate.

Redundancy

Duplication and verbosity in English is the use of two or more words that clearly mean the same thing, making one of them unnecessary. It is easy to do use redundant expressions or phrases in a conversation where speech is spontaneous, and common in spoken English. In written English, however, redundancy is more serious and harder to ignore. Here are list of redundant phrases to avoid.

1. Suddenly exploded.

An explosion is instantaneous or immediate and that is sudden enough. No need to use 'suddenly' along with exploded.

2. Final outcome.

An outcome refers to the result. An outcome is intrinsically final and so no need to use final along with outcome.

3. Advance notice/planning/reservations/ warning.

A warning, notice, reservation or plan is made before an event. Once the reader sees any of these words, they know that they were done or carried out before the event. These words do not need to be used with advance.

4. First began, new beginning.

Beginning signals the start or the first time, and therefore the use of "new" is superfluous.

5. Add an additional.

The word 'add' indicates the provision of another something, and so "additional" is superfluous.

6. For a period/number of days.

The word "days" is already in plural and clearly signifies more than just one day. It is thus redundant to use "a number of," or "a period of" along with days. Simply state the number of days or of the specific number of days is unknown, you say 'many days.'

7. Foreign imports.

Imports are foreign as they come from another country, so it is superfluous to refer to imports as "foreign."

8. Forever and ever.

Forever indicates eternity and so there is no need for "ever" as it simply duplicated forever.

9. Came at a time when.

"At a time" is not necessary in this phrase because the 'when' already provides a temporal reference to the action, coming.

10. Free gift.

It cannot be a gift if it is paid for. A gift, by nature, is free and so referring to a gift is free is redundant.

11. Collaborate/join/meet/merge together.

The words merge, join, meet and collaborate already suggest people or things coming together. It is unnecessary to use any of these words with together, such as saying merge together or join together. The correct expression is to simply say join or merge, omitting the together.

12. Invited guests.

Guests are those invited for an event. Since they had to be invited to be guests, there is no need to use invited with guests.

13. Major breakthrough.

A breakthrough is significant by nature. It can only be described as a breakthrough when there is a notable progress. The significant nature of the progress is already implied when you use the word "breakthrough," so "major" is redundant.

14. Absolutely certain or sure/essential/ guaranteed.

When someone or something is said to be sure or certain it indicates that it is without doubt. Using "absolutely" in addition to certain or sure is unnecessary. Essential or guaranteed is used for something that is absolute and so also does not need the word absolutely to accompany them.

15. Ask a question.

Ask means to present a question. Using "question" in addition to "ask" is redundant.

16. Basic fundamentals/essentials.

Using basic here is redundant. Essentials and fundamental suggest an elementary nature.

17. [Number] a.m. in the morning/p.m. in the evening.

When you write 8 a.m. the reader knows you mean 8 o'clock in the morning. It is not necessary to say 8 a.m. in the morning. Simply write 8 a.m. or 8 p.m.

18. Definite decision.

A decision is already definite even if it can be reversed later. A decision is a definite course of action has been chosen. No need to use the word definite along with the word decision.

19. Past history/record.

A record or history by definition refers to past events or occurrences. Using past to qualify history or record is unnecessary.

20. Consensus of opinion.

Consensus means agreement over something that may be or not be an opinion. So it may look that using the phrase 'consensus of opinion' is appropriate, but it is better to omit "opinion."

21. Enter in.

Enter means going in, as no one enters out. There fore no need to add "in," simply use "enter."

22. Plan ahead.

You cannot plan for the past. Planning can only be done for the future. When you use "plan," the future is already implied.

23. Possibly might.

The words might and possibly signify probability, so just use one at a time.

24. Direct confrontation.

A confrontation is a head-on conflict, and does not need to be modified with "direct."

25. Postpone until later.

Something postponed is delayed or moved to a later time, and does not need to be modified with "later."

26. False pretense.

The word pretense is only used to describe a deception, so a "false" pretense is redundant.

27. Protest against.

Protest involves showing opposition; there is no need to use against.

28. End result.

Result only comes at the end. The reader who sees the word 'result' already knows that it occurs at the end.

29. Estimated at about/roughly.

Estimates are approximations that are not expected to be accurate, and do not need to be modified with "roughly" or "about."

30. Repeat again.

Repeat refers to something done again and does not need to be modified with "again."

31. Difficult dilemma.

A dilemma is a situation that is complicated or difficult, and does not need to be modified with "difficult."

32. Revert back.

Revert indicates returning to a former or earlier state. Something that reverts goes back to how it used to be. No need to add back.

33. (During the) course (of).

During means "in or throughout the duration of," and doesn't require the use of the word "course."

34. Same identical.

Same and identical means the same thing and should not be used together.

35. Completely filled/finished/opposite.

Completely indicates thoroughness. However, the words finished and filled already indicate something thoroughly filled or finished to the extent possible. The words filled and finished thus do not need to be qualified with "completely."

36. Since the time when.

In this phrase, 'the time when' is not necessary as 'since' already indicates sometime in the past.

37. Close proximity/scrutiny.

Proximity means being close, in respect to location. Scrutiny means studying something closely. Both words already suggest close, whether in respect to location as with proximity, or in respect to study, as with scrutiny. It is therefore unnecessary to use the words together.

38. Spell out in detail.

'Spell out' involves providing details, so no need to add "in detail."

39. Written down.

Anything written can be said to be taken down. Written should therefore be used on its own.

40. (Filled to) capacity.

Anything that is filled has reached its capacity and so the word capacity does not need to be used along with filled.

41. Unintended mistake.

Something is a mistake because it is not intended. The lack

of intention is plain and so there is no need to qualify with "unintended."

42. Still remains.

"Remains" signifies that something is still as it is, and so using 'still' is superfluous.

43. Actual experience/fact.

Something becomes an experience after it has occurred. If it didn't occur it is not an experience. A fact can only be a fact when it is sure or confirmed. Both experience and fact thus do not need to be modified with "actual."

44. Therapeutic treatment.

Therapeutic refers to the healing or curing of illness. By nature all medical treatment is therapeutic in that it aims to heal or cure. When speaking of medical treatment, there is thus no need to use therapeutic to qualify treatment.

45. At the present time.

"At present" alone indicates the present time or "at this time." Using "at the present time" is the verbose version. Better to just use "at present."

46. Unexpected surprise.

A surprise is unexpected by nature. The unexpected nature is assumed once the word surprised is read or heard. No need to use unexpected to qualify it.

47. As for example.

"As" indicates the use of an example and so it is redundant to say "an example."

48. Usual custom.

A custom refers to something that is observed or done repeatedly or routinely. The use of 'usual' along with custom is not necessary.

49. Added bonus.

Bonus already indicates something extra, in addition to the ordinary. Using "added" to describe the bonus is not necessary.

50. Few in number.

Something is few because it is small in number. No need to use number with few.

Practice Test Questions Set 1

The questions below are not the same as you will find on the CAHSEE - that would be too easy! And nobody knows what the questions will be and they change all the time. Below are general questions that cover the same subject areas as the CAHSEE. So, while the format and exact wording of the questions may differ slightly, and change from year to year, if you can answer the questions below, you will have no problem with the CAHSEE.

For the best results, take these practice test questions as if it were the real exam. Set aside time when you will not be disturbed, and a location that is quiet and free of distractions. Read the instructions carefully, read each question carefully, and answer to the best of your ability.
Use the bubble answer sheets provided. When you have completed the practice questions, check your answer against the Answer Key and read the explanation provided.

Do not attempt more than one set of practice test questions in one day. After completing the first practice test, wait two or three days before attempting the second set of questions.

Reading Answer Sheet

1. A B C D
2. A B C D
3. A B C D
4. A B C D
5. A B C D
6. A B C D
7. A B C D
8. A B C D
9. A B C D
10. A B C D
11. A B C D
12. A B C D
13. A B C D
14. A B C D
15. A B C D
16. A B C D
17. A B C D
18. A B C D
19. A B C D
20. A B C D
21. A B C D
22. A B C D
23. A B C D
24. A B C D
25. A B C D
26. A B C D
27. A B C D
28. A B C D
29. A B C D
30. A B C D

Mathematics Answer Sheet

1. A B C D
2. A B C D
3. A B C D
4. A B C D
5. A B C D
6. A B C D
7. A B C D
8. A B C D
9. A B C D
10. A B C D
11. A B C D
12. A B C D
13. A B C D
14. A B C D
15. A B C D
16. A B C D
17. A B C D
18. A B C D
19. A B C D
20. A B C D
21. A B C D
22. A B C D
23. A B C D
24. A B C D
25. A B C D
26. A B C D
27. A B C D
28. A B C D
29. A B C D
30. A B C D
31. A B C D
32. A B C D
33. A B C D
34. A B C D
35. A B C D
36. A B C D
37. A B C D
38. A B C D
39. A B C D
40. A B C D
41. A B C D
42. A B C D
43. A B C D
44. A B C D
45. A B C D
46. A B C D
47. A B C D
48. A B C D
49. A B C D
50. A B C D

Essay Revision - English Grammar and Usage Answer Sheet

1. Ⓐ Ⓑ Ⓒ Ⓓ   11. Ⓐ Ⓑ Ⓒ Ⓓ   21. Ⓐ Ⓑ Ⓒ Ⓓ

2. Ⓐ Ⓑ Ⓒ Ⓓ   12. Ⓐ Ⓑ Ⓒ Ⓓ   22. Ⓐ Ⓑ Ⓒ Ⓓ

3. Ⓐ Ⓑ Ⓒ Ⓓ   13. Ⓐ Ⓑ Ⓒ Ⓓ   23. Ⓐ Ⓑ Ⓒ Ⓓ

4. Ⓐ Ⓑ Ⓒ Ⓓ   14. Ⓐ Ⓑ Ⓒ Ⓓ   24. Ⓐ Ⓑ Ⓒ Ⓓ

5. Ⓐ Ⓑ Ⓒ Ⓓ   15. Ⓐ Ⓑ Ⓒ Ⓓ   25. Ⓐ Ⓑ Ⓒ Ⓓ

6. Ⓐ Ⓑ Ⓒ Ⓓ   16. Ⓐ Ⓑ Ⓒ Ⓓ   26. Ⓐ Ⓑ Ⓒ Ⓓ

7. Ⓐ Ⓑ Ⓒ Ⓓ   17. Ⓐ Ⓑ Ⓒ Ⓓ   27. Ⓐ Ⓑ Ⓒ Ⓓ

8. Ⓐ Ⓑ Ⓒ Ⓓ   18. Ⓐ Ⓑ Ⓒ Ⓓ   28. Ⓐ Ⓑ Ⓒ Ⓓ

9. Ⓐ Ⓑ Ⓒ Ⓓ   19. Ⓐ Ⓑ Ⓒ Ⓓ   29. Ⓐ Ⓑ Ⓒ Ⓓ

10. Ⓐ Ⓑ Ⓒ Ⓓ   20. Ⓐ Ⓑ Ⓒ Ⓓ   30. Ⓐ Ⓑ Ⓒ Ⓓ

Part 1 - Reading

Questions 1 – 4 refer to the following passage.

Infectious Diseases

An infectious disease is a clinically evident illness resulting from the presence of pathogenic agents, such as viruses, bacteria, fungi, protozoa, multi-cellular parasites, and unusual proteins known as prions. Infectious pathologies are also called communicable diseases or transmissible diseases, due to their potential of transmission from one person or species to another by a replicating agent (as opposed to a toxin).

Transmission of an infectious disease can occur in many different ways. Physical contact, liquids, food, body fluids, contaminated objects, and airborne inhalation can all transmit infecting agents.

Transmissible diseases that occur through contact with an ill person, or objects touched by them, are especially infective, and are sometimes called contagious diseases. Communicable diseases that require a more specialized route of infection, such as through blood or needle transmission, or sexual transmission, are usually not regarded as contagious.

The term infectivity describes the ability of an organism to enter, survive and multiply in the host, while the infectiousness of a disease indicates the comparative ease with which the disease is transmitted. An infection however, is not synonymous with an infectious disease, as an infection may not cause important clinical symptoms. [3]

Practice Test Questions 1

1. What can we infer from the first paragraph in this passage?

    a. Sickness from a toxin can be easily transmitted from one person to another.

    b. Sickness from an infectious disease can be easily transmitted from one person to another.

    c. Few sicknesses are transmitted from one person to another.

    d. Infectious diseases are easily treated.

2. What are two other names for infections' pathologies?

    a. Communicable diseases or transmissible diseases

    b. Communicable diseases or terminal diseases

    c. Transmissible diseases or preventable diseases

    d. Communicative diseases or unstable diseases

3. What does infectivity describe?

    a. The inability of an organism to multiply in the host.

    b. The inability of an organism to reproduce.

    c. The ability of an organism to enter, survive and multiply in the host.

    d. The ability of an organism to reproduce in the host.

4. How do we know an infection is not synonymous with an infectious disease?

    a. Because an infectious disease destroys infections with enough time.

    b. Because an infection may not cause clinical symptoms or impair host function.

    c. We do not. The two are synonymous.

    d. Because an infection is too fatal to be an infectious disease.

Questions 5 – 7 refer to the following passage.

Thunderstorms

The first stage of a thunderstorm is the cumulus stage, or developing stage. In this stage, masses of moisture are lifted upwards into the atmosphere. The trigger for this lift can be insulation heating the ground producing thermals, areas where two winds converge, forcing air upwards, or where winds blow over terrain of increasing elevation. Moisture in the air rapidly cools into liquid drops of water, which appears as cumulus clouds.

As the water vapor condenses into liquid, latent heat is released which warms the air, causing it to become less dense than the surrounding dry air. The warm air rises in an updraft through the process of convection (hence the term convective precipitation). This creates a low-pressure zone beneath the forming thunderstorm. In a typical thunderstorm, about 5×10^8 kg of water vapor is lifted, and the quantity of energy released when this condenses is about equal to the energy used by a city of 100,000 in a month. [4]

5. The cumulus stage of a thunderstorm is the

    a. The last stage of the storm.
    b. The middle stage of the storm formation.
    c. The beginning of the thunderstorm.
    d. The period after the thunderstorm has ended.

6. One of the ways the air is warmed is

    a. Air moving downwards, which creates a high-pressure zone.
    b. Air cooling and becoming less dense, causing it to rise.
    c. Moisture moving downward toward the earth.
    d. Heat created by water vapor condensing into liquid.

7. Identify the correct sequence of events.

   a. Warm air rises, water droplets condense, creating more heat, and the air rises farther.

   b. Warm air rises and cools, water droplets condense, causing low pressure.

   c. Warm air rises and collects water vapor, the water vapor condenses as the air rises, which creates heat, and causes the air to rise farther.

   d. None of the above.

Questions 8 – 10 refer to the following passage.

The US Weather Service

The United States National Weather Service classifies thunderstorms as severe when they reach a predetermined level. Usually, this means the storm is strong enough to inflict wind or hail damage. In most of the United States, a storm is considered severe if winds reach over 50 knots (58 mph or 93 km/h), hail is ¾ inch (2 cm) diameter or larger, or if meteorologists report funnel clouds or tornadoes. In the Central Region of the United States National Weather Service, the hail threshold for a severe thunderstorm is 1 inch (2.5 cm) in diameter. Though a funnel cloud or tornado indicates the presence of a severe thunderstorm, the various meteorological agencies would issue a tornado warning rather than a severe thunderstorm warning.

Meteorologists in Canada define a severe thunderstorm as either having tornadoes, wind gusts of 90 km/h or greater, hail 2 centimeters in diameter or greater, rainfall more than 50 millimeters in 1 hour, or 75 millimeters in 3 hours.

Severe thunderstorms can develop from any type of thunderstorm. [5]

8. What is the purpose of this passage?

   a. Explaining when a thunderstorm turns into a tornado.

   b. Explaining who issues storm warnings, and when these warnings should be issued.

   c. Explaining when meteorologists consider a thunderstorm severe.

   d. None of the above.

9. It is possible to infer from this passage that

   a. Different areas and countries have different criteria for determining a severe storm.

   b. Thunderstorms can include lightning and tornadoes, as well as violent winds and large hail.

   c. If someone spots both a thunderstorm and a tornado, meteorological agencies will immediately issue a severe storm warning.

   d. Canada has a different alert system for severe storms, with criteria that are far less.

10. What would the Central Region of the United States National Weather Service do if hail was 2.7 cm in diameter?

   a. Not issue a severe thunderstorm warning.

   b. Issue a tornado warning.

   c. Issue a severe thunderstorm warning.

   d. Sleet must also accompany the hail before the Weather Service will issue a storm warning.

Contents

Science Self-assessment 81
Answer Key 91
Science Tutorials 96
Scientific Method 96
Biology 99
Heredity: Genes and Mutation 104
Classification 108
Ecology 110
Chemistry 112
Energy: Kinetic and Mechanical 126
Energy: Work and Power 130
Force: Newton's Three Laws 132

11. Consider the table of contents above. What page would you find information about natural selection and adaptation?

a. 81
b. 90
c. 110
d. 132

Questions 12 – 14 refer to the following passage.

Clouds

A cloud is a visible mass of droplets or frozen crystals floating in the atmosphere above the surface of the Earth or other planetary bodies. Another type of cloud is a mass of material in space, attracted by gravity, called interstellar clouds and nebulae. The branch of meteorology which studies clouds is called nephrology. When we are speaking of Earth clouds, water vapor is usually the condensing substance, which forms small droplets or ice crystal. These crystals are typically 0.01 mm in diameter. Dense, deep clouds reflect most light, so they appear white, at least from the top. Cloud droplets scatter light very efficiently, so the farther into a cloud light travels, the weaker it gets. This accounts for the gray or dark appearance at the base of large clouds. Thin clouds may appear to have acquired the color of their environment or background. [6]

12. What are clouds made of?

    a. Water droplets

    b. Ice crystals

    c. Ice crystals and water droplets

    d. Clouds on Earth are made of ice crystals and water droplets

13. The main idea of this passage is

    a. Condensation occurs in clouds, having an intense effect on the weather on the surface of the earth.

    b. Atmospheric gases are responsible for the gray color of clouds just before a severe storm happens.

    c. A cloud is a visible mass of droplets or frozen crystals floating in the atmosphere above the surface of the Earth or other planetary body.

    d. Clouds reflect light in varying amounts and degrees, depending on the size and concentration of the water droplets.

14. Why are clouds white on top and grey on the bottom?

    a. Because water droplets inside the cloud do not reflect light, it appears white, and the farther into the cloud the light travels, the less light is reflected making the bottom appear dark.

    b. Because water droplets outside the cloud reflect light, it appears dark, and the farther into the cloud the light travels, the more light is reflected making the bottom appear white.

    c. Because water droplets inside the cloud reflects light, making it appear white, and the farther into the cloud the light travels, the more light is reflected making the bottom appear dark.

    d. None of the above.

Questions 15 - 18 refer to the following recipe.

Chocolate Chip Cookies

3/4 cup sugar
3/4 cup packed brown sugar
1 cup butter, softened
2 large eggs, beaten
1 teaspoon vanilla extract
2 1/4 cups all-purpose flour
1 teaspoon baking soda
3/4 teaspoon salt
2 cups semisweet chocolate chips
If desired, 1 cup chopped pecans, or chopped walnuts.
Preheat oven to 375 degrees.

Mix sugar, brown sugar, butter, vanilla and eggs in a large bowl. Stir in flour, baking soda, and salt. The dough will be very stiff.

Stir in chocolate chips by hand with a sturdy wooden spoon. Add the pecans, or other nuts, if desired. Stir until the chocolate chips and nuts are evenly dispersed.

Drop dough by rounded tablespoonfuls 2 inches apart onto a cookie sheet.

Bake 8 to 10 minutes or, until light brown. Cookies may look underdone, but they will finish cooking after you take them out of the oven.

15. What is the correct order for adding these ingredients?

    a. Brown sugar, baking soda, chocolate chips
    b. Baking soda, brown sugar, chocolate chips
    c. Chocolate chips, baking soda, brown sugar
    d. Baking soda, chocolate chips, brown sugar

16. What does sturdy mean?

   a. Long
   b. Strong
   c. Short
   d. Wide

17. What does disperse mean?

   a. Scatter
   b. To form a ball
   c. To stir
   d. To beat

18. When can you stop stirring the nuts?

   a. When the cookies are cooked.
   b. When the nuts are evenly distributed.
   c. As soon as the nuts are added.
   d. After the chocolate chips are added.

Questions 19 – 20 refer to the following email.

SUBJECT: MEDICAL STAFF CHANGES

To all staff:

This email is to advise you of a paper on recommended medical staff changes has been posted to the Human Resources website.

The contents are of primary interest to medical staff, other staff may be interested in reading it, particularly those in medical support roles.

The paper deals with several major issues:

   1. Improving our ability to attract top quality staff to the hospital, and retain our existing staff. These changes

will make our position and departmental names internationally recognizable and comparable with North American and North Asian departments and positions.

2. Improving our ability to attract top quality staff by introducing greater flexibility in the departmental structure.

3. General comments on issues to be further discussed in relation to research staff.

The changes outlined in this paper are significant. I encourage you to read the document and send to me any comments you may have, so that it can be enhanced and improved.

Gordon Simms
Administrator,
Seven Oaks Regional Hospital

19. Are all hospital staff required to read the document posted to the Human Resources website?

    a. Yes all staff are required to read the document.

    b. No, reading the document is optional.

    c. Only medical staff are required to read the document.

    d. none of the above are correct.

20. Have the changes to medical staff been made?

    a. Yes, the changes have been made.

    b. No, the changes are only being discussed.

    c. Some of the changes have been made.

    d. None of the choices are correct.

Questions 21 – 25 refer to the following passage.

Navy Seals

The United States Navy's Sea, Air and Land Teams, commonly known as Navy SEALs, are the U.S. Navy's principle special operations force, and a part of the Naval Special Warfare Command (NSWC) as well as the maritime component of the United States Special Operations Command (USSOCOM).

The unit's acronym ("SEAL") comes from their capacity to operate at sea, in the air, and on land – but it is their ability to work underwater that separates SEALs from most other military units in the world. Navy SEALs are trained and have been deployed in a wide variety of missions, including direct action and special reconnaissance operations, unconventional warfare, foreign internal defence, hostage rescue, counter-terrorism and other missions. All SEALs are members of either the United States Navy or the United States Coast Guard.

In the early morning of May 2, 2011 local time, a team of 40 CIA-led Navy SEALs completed an operation to kill Osama bin Laden in Abbottabad, Pakistan about 35 miles (56 km) from Islamabad, the country's capital. The Navy SEALs were part of the Naval Special Warfare Development Group, previously called "Team 6." President Barack Obama later confirmed the death of bin Laden. The unprecedented media coverage raised the public profile of the SEAL community, particularly the counter-terrorism specialists commonly known as SEAL Team 6. [7]

21. Are Navy SEALs part of USSOCOM?

    a. Yes

    b. No

    c. Only for special operations

    d. No, they are part of the US Navy

22. What separates Navy SEALs from other military units?

   a. Belonging to NSWC
   b. Direct action and special reconnaissance operations
   c. Working underwater
   d. Working for other military units in the world

23. What other military organizations do SEALs belong to?

   a. The US Navy
   b. The Coast Guard
   c. The US Army
   d. The Navy and the Coast Guard

24. What other organization participated in the Bin Laden raid?

   a. The CIA
   b. The US Military
   c. Counter-terrorism specialists
   d. None of the above

25. What is the new name for Team 6?

   a. They were always called Team 6
   b. The counter-terrorism specialists
   c. The Naval Special Warfare Development Group
   d. None of the above

Questions 26 – 28 refer to the following passage.

How To Get A Good Nights Sleep

Sleep is just as essential for healthy living as water, air and food. Sleep allows the body to rest and replenish depleted energy levels. Sometimes we may for various reasons experience difficulty sleeping which has a serious effect on our health. Those who have prolonged sleeping problems are facing a serious medical condition and should see a qualified doctor as soon as possible for help. Here is simple guide that can help you sleep better at night.

Try to create a natural pattern of waking up and sleeping around the same time everyday. This means avoiding going to bed too early and oversleeping past your usual wake up time. Going to bed and getting up at radically different times everyday confuses your body clock. Try to establish a natural rhythm as much as you can.

Exercises and a bit of physical activity can help you sleep better at night. If you are having problem sleeping, try to be as active as you can during the day. If you are tired from physical activity, falling asleep is a natural and easy process for your body. If you remain inactive during the day, you will find it harder to sleep properly at night. Try walking, jogging, swimming or simple stretches as you get close to your bed time.

Afternoon naps are great to refresh you during the day, but they may also keep you awake at night. If you feel sleepy during the day, get up, take a walk and get busy to keep from sleeping. Stretching is a good way to increase blood flow to the brain and keep you alert so that you don't sleep during the day. This will help you sleep better night.

> A warm bath or a glass of milk in the evening can help your body relax and prepare for sleep. A cold bath will wake you up and keep you up for several hours. Also avoid eating too late before bed.

26. How would you describe this sentence?

    a. A recommendation

    b. An opinion

    c. A fact

    d. A diagnosis

27. Which of the following is an alternative title for this article?

    a. Exercise and a good night's sleep

    b. Benefits of a good night's sleep

    c. Tips for a good night's sleep

    d. Lack of sleep is a serious medical condition

28. Which of the following can not be inferred from this article?

    a. Biking is helpful for getting a good night's sleep.

    b. Mental activity is helpful for getting a good night's sleep.

    c. Eating bedtime snacks is not recommended.

    d. Getting up at the same time is helpful for a good night's sleep.

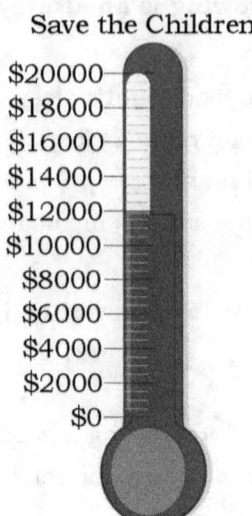

Save the Children

29. Consider the graphic above. The Save the Children fund has a fund-raising goal of $20,000. Approximately how much of their goal have they achieved?

    a. 3/5
    b. 3/4
    c. 1/2
    d. 1/3

30. Consider the graphic above. The Save the Children fund has a fund-raising goal of $16,000. Approximately how much of their goal have they achieved?

    a. 3/5
    b. 3/4
    c. 1/2
    d. 1/3

Mathematics

1. 9,177 + 7,204 =

    a. 16,4712
    b. 16,371
    c. 16,381
    d. 15,412

2. Brad has agreed to buy everyone a Coke. Each drink costs $1.89, and there are 5 friends. Estimate Brad's cost.

    a. $7
    b. $8
    c. $10
    d. $12

3. 643 - 587 =

    a. 56
    b. 66
    c. 46
    d. 55

4. Divide 243 by 3^3

    a. 243
    b. 11
    c. 9
    d. 27

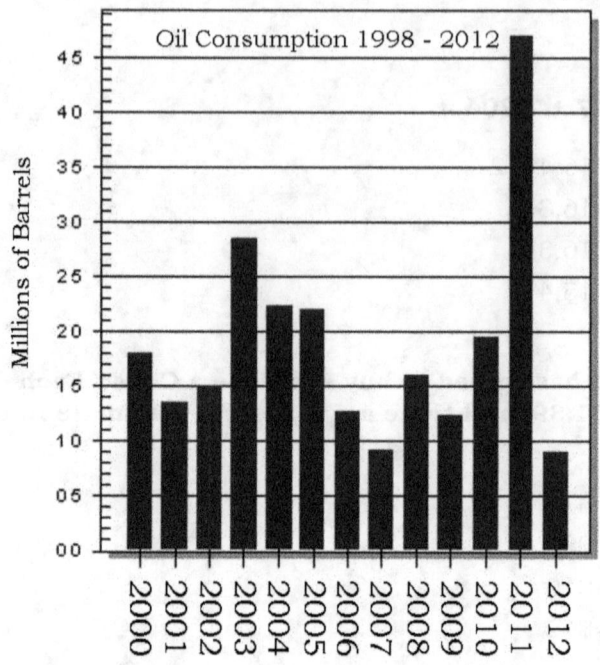

5. The graph above shows oil consumption in millions of barrels for the period, 1998 - 2012. What year did oil consumption peak?

    a. 2011
    b. 2010
    c. 2008
    d. 2009

6. Sarah weighs 25 pounds more than Tony does. If together they weigh 205 pounds, how much does Sarah weigh approximately in kilograms? Assume 1 pound = 0.4535 kilograms.

    a. 41
    b. 48
    c. 50
    d. 52

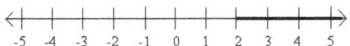

7. Choose the expression the figure represents.

    a. X ≤ 1
    b. X < 1
    c. X > 1
    d. X ≥ 1

8. Calculate (14 + 2) x 2 + 3

    a. 21
    b. 35
    c. 80
    d. 43

9. What fraction of $1500 is $75?

    a. 1/14
    b. 3/5
    c. 7/10
    d. 1/20

10. Find x and y in the following system of equations:

2x + 3 = y + 6
-4x - 12 = -8y

    a. (3,2)
    b. (1,3)
    c. (3,3)
    d. (2,2)

11. 491 ÷ 9 =

    a. 54 r5

    b. 56 r6

    c. 57 r5

    d. 51 r3

12. Below is the attendance for a class of 45.

Day	Number of Absent Students
Monday	5
Tuesday	9
Wednesday	4
Thursday	10
Friday	6

What is the average attendance for the week?

    a. 88%

    b. 85%

    c. 81%

    d. 77%

13. John purchased a jacket at a 7% discount. He had a membership which gave him an additional 2% discount on the discounted price. If he paid $425, what is the retail price of the jacket?

    a. $460

    b. $466

    c. $466

    d. $472

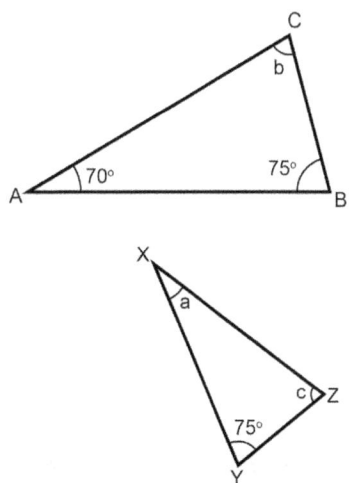

14. What are the respective values of a, b & c if both triangles are similar?

    a. 70°, 70°, 35°
    b. 70°, 35°, 70°
    c. 35°, 35°, 35°
    d. 70°, 35°, 35°

15. $7^5 - 3^5 =$

    a. 15,000
    b. 15,807
    c. 15,800
    d. 15,007

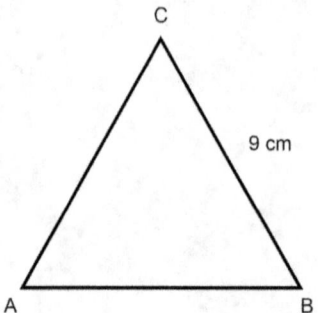

16. What is the perimeter of the equilateral △ABC above?

    a. 18 cm
    b. 12 cm
    c. 27 cm
    d. 15 cm

17. Consider 2 triangles, ABC and A'B'C', where:

    BC = B' C'
    AC = A' C'
    RA = RA'

Are these 2 triangles congruent?

    a. Yes
    b. No
    c. Not enough information

18. **Convert from scientific notation: 5.63 x 10^6**

    a. 5,630,000
    b. 563,000
    c. 5630
    d. 0.000005.630

19. **Solve the following equation 4(y + 6) = 3y + 30**

    a. y = 20
    b. y = 6
    c. y = 30/7
    d. y = 30

20. **10 x 2 − (7 + 9)**

    a. 21
    b. 16
    c. 4
    d. 13

21. **A map uses a scale of 1:2,000   How much distance on the ground is 5.2 inches on the map if the scale is in inches?**

    a. 100,400
    b. 10, 500
    c. 10,400
    d. 1,400

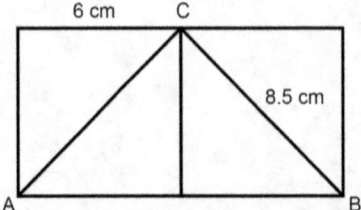

Note: figure not drawn to scale

22. Assuming the quadrangles are identical rectangles, what is the perimeter of △ABC in the above shape?

   a. 25.5 cm
   b. 27 cm
   c. 30 cm
   d. 29 cm

23. Solve for x if, $10^2 \times 100^2 = 1000^x$

   a. x = 2
   b. x = 3
   c. x = -2
   d. x = 0

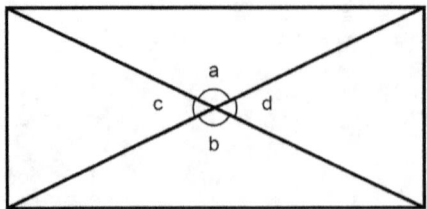

24. What is the sum of angles a, b, c and d in the rectangle above?

   a. 180°
   b. 360°
   c. 90°
   d. 120°

25. Express 5 x 5 x 5 x 5 x 5 x 5 in exponential form.

   a. 5^6
   b. 10^6
   c. 5^{16}
   d. 5^3

26. 1278 + 4920 =

   a. 6298
   b. 6108
   c. 6198
   d. 6098

27. A shop sells a piece of equipment for $545. If 15% of the cost was added to the price as value added tax, what is the actual cost of the equipment?

   a. $490.40
   b. $473.91
   c. $505.00
   d. $503.15

28. Express 9 x 9 x 9 in exponential form and standard form.

   a. $9^3 = 719$
   b. $9^3 = 629$
   c. $9^3 = 729$
   d. $10^3 = 729$

29. 5 men have to share a load weighing 10 kg 550 g equally among themselves. How much weight will each man have to carry?

    a. 900 g
    b. 1.5 kg
    c. 3 kg
    d. 2 kg 110 g

30. Divide 0.524 by 10^3

    a. 0.0524
    b. 0.000524
    c. 0.00524
    d. 524

31. Find the solution for the following linear equation: 5x/2 = (3x + 24)/6.

    a. -1
    b. 0
    c. 1
    d. 2

32. $3^2 \times 3^5$

    a. 3^{17}
    b. 3^5
    c. 4^8
    d. 3^7

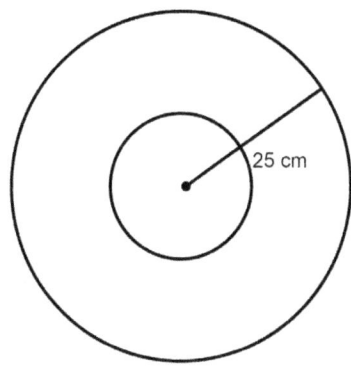

Note: figure not drawn to scale

33. What is the distance travelled by the wheel above, when it makes 175 revolutions?

    a. 87.5 π m
    b. 875 π m
    c. 8.75 π m
    d. 8750 π m

34. 7130 − 2136 =

    a. 4909
    b. 4994
    c. 4494
    d. 4954

35. A woman spent 15% of her income on an item and ends up with $120. What percentage of her income is left?

    a. 12%
    b. 85%
    c. 75%
    d. 95%

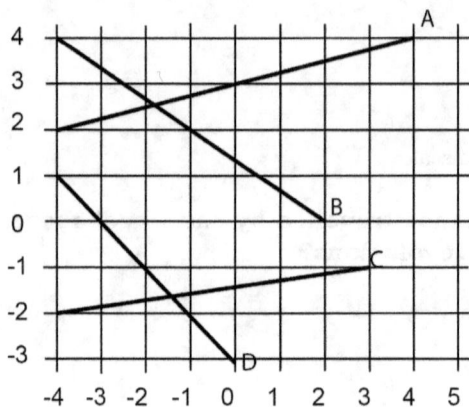

36. Which of the lines above represents the equation 2y − x = 4?

    a. A
    b. B
    c. C
    d. D

37. 1440 ÷ 12 =

    a. 122
    b. 120
    c. 110
    d. 132

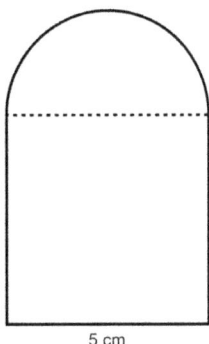

5 cm

38. What is the perimeter of the above shape?

    a. 17.5 π cm

    b. 20 π cm

    c. 15 π cm

    d. 25 π cm

39. A square lawn has an area of 62,500 square meters. What is the cost of building fence around it at a rate of $5.5 per meter?

    a. $4,000

    b. $5,500

    c. $4,500

    d. $5,000

40. Solve $3^5 \div 3^8$

    a. 3^3

    b. 3^5

    c. 3^6

    d. 3^4

41. Find the sides of a right triangle whose sides are consecutive numbers.

    a. 1, 2, 3
    b. 2, 3, 4
    c. 3, 4, 5
    d. 4, 5, 6

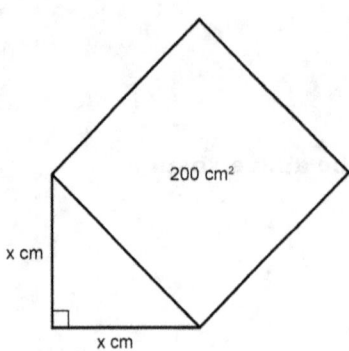

Note: figure not drawn to scale

42. Assuming the quadrangle is square, what is the length of the sides in the triangle above?

    a. 10
    b. 20
    c. 100
    d. 40

43. Solve the linear equation: $3(x + 2) - 2(1 - x) = 4x + 5$

    a. -1
    b. 0
    c. 1
    d. 2

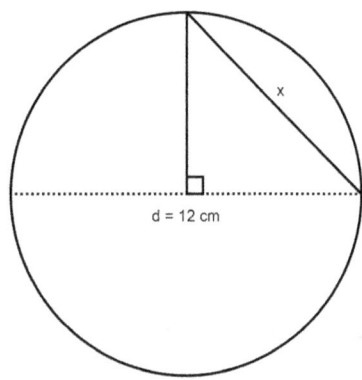

Note: figure not drawn to scale

44. Calculate the length of side x.

    a. 6.46
    b. 8.46
    c. 3.6
    d. 6.4

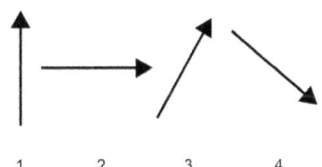

1   2   3   4

45. What is the correct order of respective slopes for the lines above?

    a. Positive, undefined, negative, positive
    b. Negative, zero, undefined, positive
    c. Undefined, zero, positive, negative
    d. Zero, positive undefined, negative

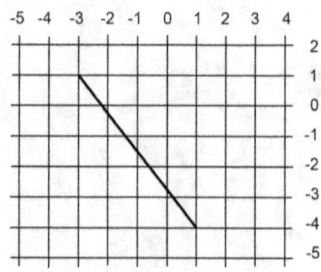

46. What is the slope of the line shown above?

   a. 5/4
   b. -4/5
   c. -5/4
   d. -4/5

47. Convert 0.045 to scientific notation.

   a. 4.5×10^{-2}
   b. 4.5×10^{2}
   c. 4.05×10^{-2}
   d. 4.5×10^{-3}

48. 5575 + 8791 =

   a. 14,756
   b. 14,566
   c. 14,466
   d. 14,366

49. A mother is 7 times older than her child. In 25 years, her age will be double that of her child. How old is the mother now?

    a. 35
    b. 33
    c. 30
    d. 25

50. In a grade 8 exam, students are asked to divide a number by 3/2, but a student mistakenly multiplied the number by 3/2 and the answer is 5 more than the required one. What was the number?

    a. 4
    b. 5
    c. 6
    d. 8

English Grammar and Usage

1. Thomas Edison _____ since he invented the light bulb, television, motion pictures, and phonograph.

    a. has always been known as the greatest inventor
    b. was always been known as the greatest inventor
    c. must have had been always known as the greatest inventor
    d. will had been known as the greatest inventor

2. Although Joe is tall for his age, his brother Elliot is _____ of the two.

    a. the tallest
    b. more tallest
    c. the tall
    d. the taller

3. When KISS came to town, all of the tickets _____ before I could buy one.

    a. will be sold out

    b. had been sold out

    c. were being sold out

    d. was sold out

4. The rules of most sports _____ more complicated than we often realize.

    a. are

    b. is

    c. was

    d. has been

5. _____ won first place in the Western Division?

    a. Who

    b. Whom

    c. Which

    d. What

6. There are now several ways to listen to music, including radio, CDs, and Mp3 files _____ you can download onto an MP3 player.

    a. on which

    b. who

    c. whom

    d. which

7. Choose the correct sentence.

a. Historians have been guessing the doctor was a woman for more than 100 years.

b. Historians have been guessing for more than 100 years the doctor was a woman.

c. Historians guessed the doctor was a woman for more than 100 years.

d. None of the above.

8. Choose the correct sentence.

a. None of us want to go to the party not even, if there will be live music.

b. None of us want to go to the party, not even if there will be live music.

c. None of us want to go to the party not even if there will be live music.

d. None of us want to go to the party; not even if there will be live music.

9. Choose the correct sentence.

a. I own two dogs, a cat named Jeffrey, and Henry, the goldfish.

b. I own two dogs a cat, named Jeffrey, and Henry, the goldfish.

c. I own two dogs, a cat named Jeffrey; and Henry, the goldfish.

d. I own two dogs, a cat, named Jeffrey and Henry, the goldfish.

10. Choose the correct sentence.

a. During the years he was President, the country fought two wars.

b. During the years he was president, the country fought two wars.

c. During the years he was president, the Country fought two wars.

d. During the years he was President, the Country fought two wars.

11. Choose the sentence with the correct grammar.

a. Don would never have thought of that book, but you could have reminded him.

b. Don would never of thought of that book, but you could have reminded him.

c. Don would never have thought of that book, but you could of have reminded him.

d. Don would never of thought of that book, but you could of reminded him.

12. Choose the correct sentence.

a. The boy and girl are related.

b. The boy and girl is related.

c. The boy and girl was related.

d. None of the above.

13. Choose the sentence with the correct grammar.

a. There was scarcely no food in the pantry, because nobody ate at home.

b. There was scarcely any food in the pantry, because nobody ate at home.

c. There was scarcely any food in the pantry, because not nobody ate at home.

d. There was scarcely no food in the pantry, because not nobody ate at home.

14. Choose the sentence with the correct grammar.

a. Its important for you to know its official name; its called the Confederate Museum.

b. It's important for you to know it's official name; it's called the Confederate Museum.

c. It's important for you to know its official name; it's called the Confederate Museum.

d. Its important for you to know it's official name; it's called the Confederate Museum.

15. Choose the sentence with the correct grammar.

a. The man as well as his son has arrived.

b. The man as well as his son have arrived.

c. Both of the above.

d. None of the above.

Essay Revision

Curiosity's Mission

Mankind's thirst for knowledge about ourselves and the universe has always been insatiable, making curiosity a driving force for human advances through history. [1] Not only that, human curiosity and creativity have created countless works of fiction that speculate about future discoveries based on the facts we know. [2]

Our neighboring planet Mars, for example, has for long lead scientists and writers to generate stories about living on the Red Planet. [3] Serious endeavors in science and technological are motivated by our never-ending questions. [4] So far, NASA has carried out several exploratory missions to Mars and the rover robot Curiosity is the latest and most sophisticated. [5]

Curiosity was launched in late November 2011 from Cape Canaveral Air Force Station in Florida. [6] It successfully landed on Mars on August 6, 2012 in search of evidence of life, if it ever existed there. [7] The car sized robot, weighing about a ton, is equipped with all the technical capacities to carry out its mission and it will be exploring our neighbor for any biological, geological and geochemical traces of life on the planet. [8] It will also try to test the Martian soil and surface to collect data about its planetary evolution and surface radiation. [9]

Curiosity has been engineered with cutting-edge technologies worth over 2.5 billion US dollars. [10] The most incredible component of the rover is the on-board science lab. [11] Apart from that, it consists of a communications system that allows transmission of commands to the rover from the control centre at NASA, enabling direct control of the robot's activities on the surface of the Red Planet. [12] The Curiosity rover has several mounted cameras which assists the rover to navigate as well as capture images from the Martian surface and transmit them back to Earth. [13] The rover is also designed to accommodate to the extreme conditions prevalent on Mars. [14]

1. How would you re-write sentence 1?

a. No changes

b. Mankind's thirst for knowledge has always been insatiable, making curiosity a driving factor for human advances through history.

c. Mankind's thirst for knowledge is insatiable, making curiosity a driving factor for human advances through history.

d. Humankind's thirst for knowledge is insatiable, making curiosity a driving force in advances throughout history.

2. Which sentence in the third paragraph is least relevant to the main idea of the third paragraph?

a. 6

b. 8

c. 9

d. 10

3. Which of the following is/are needed to sentence 5?

a. So far, "NASA" has carried out several exploration missions to Mars and the robot rover Curiosity is the latest and most sophisticated of all.

b. So far, NASA has carried out several exploration missions to Mars and the robot rover Curiosity is the latest and most sophisticated of all.

c. So far, NASA has carried out several exploration missions to Mars and the robot rover -Curiosity- is the latest and most sophisticated of all.

d. So far, NASA has carried out several exploration missions to Mars and the robot rover "Curiosity" is the latest and most sophisticated of all.

4. Which of the following changes is/are needed in sentence 5?

    a. So far, "NASA" has carried out several exploration missions to Mars and the rover robot Curiosity is the latest and most sophisticated of all.

    b. So far, NASA has carried out several exploratory missions to Mars and the rover robot Curiosity is the latest and most sophisticated of all.

    c. So far, NASA has carried out several exploration missions to Mars and the rover robot -Curiosity- is the latest and most sophisticated of all.

    d. So far, NASA has carried out several exploratory missions to Mars and the rover robot "Curiosity" is the latest and most sophisticated of all.

Green Energy from Olive Oil

The debate over developing sustainable energy sources have been very active in the past two decades. [1] With continued concern over global climate change, environmentalists are urging governments for lowering their dependence on fossil fuels in order for ensuring reduced carbon emission into the atmosphere. [2] Consequently, governments worldwide are turning their attention to the search for non-emissive sources of energy. [3] Renewable substitutes under extensive research are solar power, wind, geothermal energy and harnessing energy from ocean waves. [4]

While the search for environment friendly energy sources is already under way, developing these alternatives at a reasonable cost is a major challenge. [5] No cost-effective replacement for fossil fuels has yet been found. [6] However, recent years have seen remarkable progress in solar energy. [7] Ted Sargent, a Professor at University of Toronto, Canada, has discovered that olive oil has the capacity to capture solar radiation and emit electrons resulting in an electric current. [8] This is a major discovery in the solar power generation industry as it offers a cheap source of harnessing the Sun's energy. [9]

Oleic acid, the main ingredient of olive oil, absorbs infrared radiation is the major component of the Sun's radiation reaching the Earth. [10] The discovery is significant because, so far, no attempt has been made to use the abundant infrared radiation we receive throughout the year. [11] Infrared (IR) light is electromagnetic radiation with longer wavelengths than those of visible light. [12] Capturing this heat wave radiation, along with the photons that are present in sunlight, increases the efficiency of the solar cells that are already being manufactured commercially. [13] And to make it possible, Professor Sargent has developed a new kind of solar cell called "quantum dots," tiny cells made from gels of tin, bismuth, lead, sulphur and selenium mixed with extra pure olive oil. [14] The resulting ink-like crystal absorbs both photons and infrared radiation and has the capacity to transmit electrons and produce a current. [15]

This new method of capturing the Sun's energy is considered a breakthrough in the solar power industry as it offers cheaper alternatives to the existing use of silicon crystals which are costly to manufacture. [16] And although the invention is yet to prove it's efficiency, alot of funding has already been dedicated to further research. [17]

5. What sentence is not related to the main idea of paragraph 2?

    a. 6
    b. 10
    c. 12
    d. 13

6. Which of the following is a correct version of sentence 17?

a. And although the invention is yet to prove its efficiency in harnessing solar energy, alot of funding has already been dedicated to further research.

b. And although the invention is yet to prove it's efficiency in harnessing solar energy, a lot of funding has already been dedicated to further research.

c. And although the invention is yet to prove its efficiency in harnessing solar energy, a lot of funding has already been dedicated to further research.

d. No changes are necessary.

7. Which of the following changes are needed in sentence 10?

a. Oleic acid, the main ingredient of olive oil, absorbs infrared radiation is the major component of the Sun's radiation reaching the Earth.

b. Oleic acid, the main ingredient of olive oil, absorbs infrared radiation, which is the major component of the Sun's radiation reaching the Earth.

c. Oleic acid, the main ingredient of olive oil absorbs infrared radiation that is the major component of the Sun's radiation reaching the Earth.

d. Oleic acid, the main ingredient of olive oil, absorbs infrared radiation what is the major component of the Sun's radiation reaching the Earth.

8. Which of the following changes are needed in sentence 2?

a. With continued concern over global climate change, environmentalists are urging governments to lowering their dependence on fossil fuels to ensuring reduced carbon emission into the atmosphere.

b. With continued concern over global climate change, environmentalists are urging governments lower their dependence on fossil fuels in order for ensuring reduced carbon emission into the atmosphere.

c. With continued concern over global climate change, environmentalists are urging governments to lower their dependence on fossil fuels in order for ensuring reduced carbon emission into the atmosphere.

d. With continued concern over global climate change, environmentalists are urging governments to lower their dependence on fossil fuels to ensure reduced carbon emission into the atmosphere.

Hunting Lost Cities from Space

Satellite imaging has become widespread with improvements in telecommunication over the past two decades. [1] Communication satellites in orbit around the Earth have enabled large-scale mapping of the planet's surface which has become freely available thanks to technology giants like Google. [2] Satellite mapping has opened up new possibilities in diverse fields of science and technology. [3]

The key feature of the new tool, according to Professor Sarah Parcak, who discovered many cities, temples and pyramids covered under sands and sediment; is that it offers a wider perspective in size and scale of the location under study. [4] Along with the visual information that the satellite images provide, numerous details about the sites can be obtained from infrared (IR) and gravitational field images. [5] This information, coupled with conventional on-site procedures, are vital for archeology. [6]

IR data collected from satellite imaging provide clues about the activities of humans living in the contemporary times of their civilizations- including their agriculture, vegetation, structures, habitation roads and much more. [7] This type of information is derived from IR imagery which detects IR radiation present in sunlight as it is reflected by the Earth. [8] Different points in a civilization reflect IR radiation in different proportions, revealing the contrast between different areas and provide detailed insight about the causes of these differing heat signatures. [9]

9. Which of the following changes in sentence 6 would focus attention on the main idea of the second paragraph?

> a. These information, along with a supply of some heavy machinery, will help the excavation of every archeological site accomplished within a short period of time.
>
> b. This information, coupled with conventional on-site procedures, help archeologists plan their excavation carefully and efficiently.
>
> c. Such details are valuable records of ancient history and are essential assets of any civilization.
>
> d. Such details, unfortunately, are available to archeological firms who are willing to invest a lot of money on putting satellites into orbit.

10. What is the best way to re-write the underlined portion of sentence 6?

> a. coupled
> b. together with
> c. and
> d. or

11. Which of the following sentences, if inserted after sentence 3, would best illustrate the main idea of the passage?

a. The application has inspired archeologists to use it for searching for the traces of ancient civilizations and other anthropological dynamics.

b. The new technology will be very useful for excavation of archeological sites.

c. The application is a breakthrough for archeology and anthropology since it will allows us to zoom into the distant past to look for lost civilizations.

d. The concept has many positive aspects in archeological science and excavation.

12. Which of the following change(s) is/are needed to sentence 4?

a. The key feature of the new tool- according to Professor Sarah Parcak, who discovered many cities, temples and pyramids covered under sands and sediment- is that it offers a wider perspective in size and scale of the location.

b. The key feature of the new tool- according to Professor Sarah Parcak- who discovered many cities, temples and pyramids covered under sands and sediment, is that it offers a wider perspective in size and scale of the location under study.

c. The key feature of the new tool according to Professor Sarah Parcak- who discovered many cities, temples and pyramids covered under sands and sediment- is that it offers a wider perspective in size and scale of the location under study.

d. The key feature of the new tool, according to Professor Sarah Parcak- who discovered many cities, temples and pyramids covered under sands and sediment is that it offers a wider perspective in size and scale of the location under study.

Answer Key

Reading

1. B
We can infer from this passage that sickness from an infectious disease can be easily transmitted from one person to another.

From the passage, "Infectious pathologies are also called communicable diseases or transmissible diseases, due to their potential of transmission from one person or species to another by a replicating agent (as opposed to a toxin)."

2. A
Two other names for infectious pathologies are communicable diseases and transmissible diseases.

From the passage, "Infectious pathologies are also called communicable diseases or transmissible diseases, due to their potential of transmission from one person or species to another by a replicating agent (as opposed to a toxin)."

3. C
Infectivity describes the ability of an organism to enter, survive and multiply in the host. This is taken directly from the passage, and is a definition type question.

Definition type questions can be answered quickly and easily by scanning the passage for the word you are asked to define.

"Infectivity" is an unusual word, so it is quick and easy to scan the passage looking for this word.

4. B
We know an infection is not synonymous with an infectious disease because an infection may not cause important clinical symptoms or impair host function.

5. C
The cumulus stage of a thunderstorm is the beginning of the

thunderstorm.

This is taken directly from the passage, "The first stage of a thunderstorm is the cumulus, or developing stage."

6. D
The passage lists four ways that air is heated. One of the ways is, heat created by water vapor condensing into liquid.

7. A
The sequence of events can be taken from these sentences:

As the moisture carried by the [1] air currents rises, it rapidly cools into liquid drops of water, which appear as cumulus clouds. As the water vapor condenses into liquid, it [2] releases heat, which warms the air. This in turn causes the air to become less dense than the surrounding dry air and [3] rise further.

8. C
The purpose of this text is to explain when meteorologists consider a thunderstorm severe.

The main idea is the first sentence, "The United States National Weather Service classifies thunderstorms as severe when they reach a predetermined level." After the first sentence, the passage explains and elaborates on this idea. Everything is this passage is related to this idea, and there are no other major ideas in this passage that are central to the whole passage.

9. A
From this passage, we can infer that different areas and countries have different criteria for determining a severe storm.

From the passage we can see that most of the US has a criteria of, winds over 50 knots (58 mph or 93 km/h), and hail ¾ inch (2 cm). For the Central US, hail must be 1 inch (2.5 cm) in diameter. In Canada, winds must be 90 km/h or greater, hail 2 centimeters in diameter or greater, and rainfall more than 50 millimeters in 1 hour, or 75 millimeters in 3 hours.

Choice D is incorrect because the Canadian system is the same for hail, 2 centimeters in diameter.

10. C
With hail above the minimum size of 2.5 cm. diameter, the Central Region of the United States National Weather Service would issue a severe thunderstorm warning.

11. C
You would find information about natural selection and adaptation in the ecology section which begins on page 110.

12. D
Clouds in space are made of different materials attracted by gravity. Clouds on Earth are made of water droplets or ice crystals.

Choice D is the best answer. Notice also that Choice D is the most specific.

13. C
The main idea is the first sentence of the passage; a cloud is a visible mass of droplets or frozen crystals floating in the atmosphere above the surface of the Earth or other planetary body.

The main idea is very often the first sentence of the paragraph.

14. C
This question asks about the process, and gives choices that can be confirmed or eliminated easily.

From the passage, "Dense, deep clouds reflect most light, so they appear white, at least from the top. Cloud droplets scatter light very efficiently, so the farther into a cloud light travels, the weaker it gets. This accounts for the gray or dark appearance at the base of large clouds."

We can eliminate choice A, since water droplets inside the cloud do not reflect light is false.

We can eliminate choice B, since, water droplets outside the cloud reflect light, it appears dark, is false.

Choice C is correct.

15. A
The correct order of ingredients is brown sugar, baking soda and chocolate chips.

16. B
Sturdy: strong, solid in structure or person. In context, Stir in chocolate chips by hand with a *sturdy* wooden spoon.

17. A
Disperse: to scatter in different directions or break up. In context, Stir until the chocolate chips and nuts are evenly *dispersed*.

18. B
You can stop stirring the nuts when they are evenly distributed. From the passage, "Stir until the chocolate chips and nuts are evenly dispersed."

19. B
Reading the document posted to the Human Resources website is optional.

20. B
The document is recommended changes and have not be implemented yet.

21. A
Navy SEALS are the maritime component of the United States Special Operations Command (USSOCOM).

22. C
Working underwater separates SEALs from other military units. This is taken directly from the passage.

23. D
SEALs also belong to the Navy and the Coast Guard.

24. A
The CIA also participated. From the passage, the raid was conducted by a "team of 40 *CIA-led* Navy SEALS."

25. C
From the passage, "The Navy SEALs were part of the Naval Special Warfare Development Group, previously called "Team 6." "

26. A
The sentence is a recommendation.

27. C
Tips for a good night's sleep is the best alternative title for this article.

28. B
Mental activity is helpful for a good night's sleep is can not be inferred from this article.

29. A
The Save the Children's fund has raised $12,000 out of $20,000, or 12/20. Simplifying, 12/20 = 3/5

30. B
The Save the Children's fund has raised $12,000 out of $16,000, or 12/16. Simplifying, 12/16 = 3/4

Mathematics

1. C
9,177 + 7,204 = 1973

2. C
If there are 5 friends and each drink costs $1.89, we can round up to $2 per drink and estimate the total cost at, 5 X $2 = $10.
The actual cost is 5 X $1.89 = $9.45.

Practice Test Questions 1 243

3. A
643 - 587 =

4. C
243/3 x 3 x 3 = 243/27 = 9

5. A
The graph shows oil consumption peaked in 2011.

6. D
Let us denote Sarah's weight by "x." Then, since she weighs 25 pounds more than Tony, Tony will be x-25. They together weigh 205 pounds which means that the sum of the two representations will be equal to 205:

Sarah : x

Tony : x - 25

x + (x - 25) = 205 ... by arranging this equation we have:

x + x - 25 = 205

2x - 25 = 205 ... we add 25 to each side to have x term alone:

2x - 25 + 25 = 205 + 25

2x = 230

x = 230/2

x = 115 pounds → Sarah weighs 115 pounds. Since 1 pound is 0.4535 kilograms, we need to multiply 115 by 0.4535 to have her weight in kilograms:

x = 115 • 0.4535 = 52.1525 kilograms → this is equal to 52 when rounded to the nearest whole number.

7. B
The line is pointing towards numbers less than 1. The equation is therefore, X < 1.

8. B
(14 + 2) x 2 + 3 = 35. Order or operations, do brackets first, then multiplication and division, then addition and subtrac-

tion.

9. D
75/1500 = 15/300 = 3/60 = 1/20

10. B
(3, 3)
2x + 3 = y + 6
-4x - 12 = -8y

y = 2x + 3 - 6
y = 2x - 3
-4x - 12 = -8(2x - 3)
-4x - 12 = -16x + 24
-4x + 16 = 12 + 24
12x = 36
x = 3

y = 2x - 3
y = 2 * 3 - 3 = 3

11. A
491 ÷ 9 = 54 r5

12. B

Day	Number of Absent Students	Number of Present Students	% Attendance
Monday	5	40	88.88%
Tuesday	9	36	80.00%
Wednesday	4	41	91.11%
Thursday	10	35	77.77%
Friday	6	39	86.66%

To find the average or mean, sum the series and divide by the number of items.
88.88 + 80.00 + 91.11 + 77.77 + 86.66/5
424.42/5 = 84.88
Round up to 85%.

Percentage attendance will be 85%

13. C
Let the original price be 100x.

At the rate of 7% discount, the discount will be 100x•7/100 = 7x. So, the discounted price will be = 100x - 7x = 93x.

Over this price, at the rate of 2% additional discount, the discount will be 93x•2/100 = 1.86x. So, the additionally discounted price will be = 93x - 1.86x = 91.14x.

This is the amount which John has paid for the jacket:

91.14x = 425

x = 425 / 91.14 = 4.6631

The jacket costs 100x. So, 100x = 100•4.6631 = $466.31.

When rounded to the nearest whole number, this is equal to $466.

14. D
Comparing angles on similar triangles, a, b and c will be 70°, 35°, 35°

15. B
(7 x 7 x 7 x 7 x 7 x 7) - (10 x 10 x 10) = 16,807 – 1,000 = 15,807.

16. C
To find the perimeter of an equilateral triangle with 9 cm. sides, add the sides. 9+9+9 = 27 cm.

17. A
Yes the triangles are congruent. This is a case of SSA:

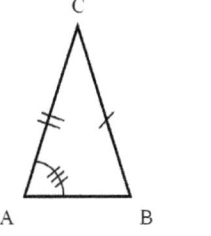
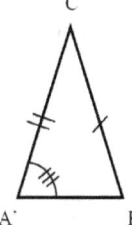

18. A
The scientific notation is in the positive so we shift the decimal 6 places to the right. Thus it is 5,630,000

19. B
$4y + 24 = 3y + 30$, $= 4y - 3y + 24 = 30$, $= y + 24 = 30$, $= y = 30 - 24$, $= y = 6$

20. C
$10 \times 2 - (7 + 9) = 4$. This is an order of operations question. Do brackets first, then multiplication and division, then addition and subtraction.

21. C
1 inch on map = 2,000 inches on ground. So, 5.2 inches on map = 5.2•2,000 = 10,400 inches on ground.

22. D
Perimeter of triangle ABC is asked.
Perimeter of a triangle = sum of all three sides.

Here, Perimeter of $\triangle ABC$ = $|AC|$ + $|CB|$ + $|AB|$.

Since the triangle is located in the middle of two adjacent and identical rectangles, we find the side lengths using these rectangles:

$|AB|$ = 6 + 6 = 12 cm

$|CB|$ = 8.5 cm

$|AC|$ = $|CB|$ = 8.5 cm

Perimeter = $|AC|$ + $|CB|$ + $|AB|$ = 8.5 + 8.5 + 12 = 29 cm

23. A
$10 \times 10 \times 100 \times 100 = 1000^x$, $=100 \times 10,000 = 1000^x$, $= 1,000,000 = 1000^x = x = 2$

24. B
$a + b + c + d = ?$
The sum of angles around a point is 360°
$a + b + c + d = 360°$

25. A
5^6

Practice Test Questions 1 247

26. C
1278 + 4920 = 6198

27. B
Actual cost = X, therefore, 545 = x + 0.15x, 545 = 1x + 0.15x, 545 = 1.15x, x = 545/1.15 = 473.9

28. C
Exponential form is 9^3 and standard from is 729

29. D
First, we need to convert all units to grams. Since 1000 g = 1 kg:

10 kg 550 g = 10•1000 g + 550 g = 10,000 g + 550 g = 10,550 g.

10,550 g is shared between 5 men. So each man will have to carry 10,550/5 = 2,110 g

2,110 g = 2,000 g + 110 g = 2 kg 110 g

30. B
0.524/ (10•10•10) = 0.524/1000 ... This means that we need to carry the decimal point 3 decimals left from the point it is now:

= 0.0.0.0.524 = 0.000524

31. D
Our aim to collect the knowns on one side and the unknowns (x terms) on the other side:

5x/2 = (3x + 24)/6 ... First, we can simplify the denominators of both sides by 2:

5x = (3x + 24)/3 ... Now, we can do cross multiplication:

15x = 3x + 24

15x - 3x = 24

12x = 24

x = 24/12 = 2

32. D
When multiplying exponents with the same base, add the exponents. $3^2 \times 3^5 = 3^{2+5} = 3^7$

33. A
The wheel travels $2\pi r$ distance when it makes one revolution. Here, r stands for the radius. The radius is given as 25 cm in the figure. So,

$2\pi r = 2\pi \cdot 25 = 50\pi$ cm is the distance travelled in one revolution.

In 175 revolutions: $175 \cdot 50\pi = 8750\pi$ cm is travelled.

We are asked to find the distance in meter.

1 m = 100 cm So;

8750π cm = 8750π / 100 = 87.5π m

34. B
7130 – 2136 = 4994

35. B
She spent 15% - 100% - 15% = 85%

36. A
If a line represents an equation, all points on that line should satisfy the equation. Meaning that all (x, y) pairs present on the line should be able to verify that 2y - x is equal to 4. We can find out the correct line by trying a (x, y) point existing on each line. It is easier to choose points on the intersection of the gridlines:
Let us try the point (4, 4) on line A:

$2 \cdot 4 - 4 = 4$

$8 - 4 = 4$

$4 = 4$ ... this is a correct result, so the equation for line A is $2y - x = 4$.

Let us try other points to check the other lines:

Point (-1, 2) on line B:

2•2 - (-1) = 4

4 + 1 = 4

5 = 4 ... this is a wrong result, so the equation for line B is not 2y - x = 4.

Point (3, -1) on line C:

2•(-1) - 3 = 4

-2 - 3 = 4

-5 = 4 ... this is a wrong result, so the equation for line C is not 2y - x = 4.

Point (-2, -1) on line D:

2•(-1) - (-2) = 4

-2 + 2 = 4

0 = 4 ... this is a wrong result, so the equation for line D is not 2y - x = 4.

37. B
1440 ÷ 12 = 120

38. A
The shape is made of a square and a semi circle. Calculate the perimeter of each and add.
Perimeter = 3 sides of the square + ½ circumference of the circle.
= (3 x 5) + ½(5 π)
= 15 + 2.5 π
Perimeter = 17.5 π cm

39. B
As the lawn is square, the length of one side will be the square root of the area. √62,500 = 250 meters. So, the perimeter is found by 4 times the length of the side of the square:

250•4 = 1000 meters.

Since each meter costs $5.5, the total cost of the fence will be 1000•5.5 = $5,500.

40. A
To divide exponents with the same base, subtract the exponents. $3^{8-5} = 3^3$

41. C
The length of the sides is, 3, 4, 5.

x
y = x + 1
z = x + 2
$x^2 + y^2 = y^2$
$x^2 + (x + 1)^2 = (x + 2)^2$
$x^2 + x^2 + 2x + 1 = x^2 + 4x + 4$
$x^2 - 2x - 3$ 0

$x_{1,2} = 2 \pm \sqrt{4 + 12} \;/\; 2$
$x_{1,2} = 2 \pm 4 \;/\; 2$

x = 3
y = 4
z = 5

42. A
If we call one side of the square "a," the area of the square will be a^2.

We know that $a^2 = 200$ cm².

On the other hand; there is an isosceles right triangle. Using the **Pythagorean Theorem:**
(Hypotenuse)² = (Perpendicular)² + (Base)²
$h^2 = a^2 + b^2$

Given: $h^2 = 200$, a = b = x
Then, $x^2 + x^2 = 200$, $2x^2 = 200$, $x^2 = 100$
x = 10

43. C
To solve the linear equation, we operate the knowns and unknowns within each other and try to obtain x term (which is the unknown) alone on one side of the equation:

3(x + 2) - 2(1 - x) = 4x + 5 ... We remove the parenthesis by distributing the factors:

3x + 6 - 2 + 2x = 4x + 5

5x + 4 = 4x + 5

5x - 4x = 5 - 4

x = 1

44. B
In the question, we have a right triangle formed inside the circle. We are asked to find the length of the hypotenuse of this triangle. We can find the other two sides of the triangle by using circle properties:

The diameter of the circle is equal to 12 cm. The legs of the right triangle are the radii of the circle; so they are 6 cm long.

Pythagorean Theorem:
(Hypotenuse)² = (Perpendicular)² + (Base)²
$h^2 = a^2 + b^2$

Given: d (diameter)= 12 & r (radius) = a = b = 6
$h^2 = a^2 + b^2$
$h^2 = 6^2 + 6^2$, $h^2 = 36 + 36$
$h^2 = 72$
h = 8.46

45. C
Undefined, zero, positive, negative.

46. C
Slope (m) = change in y / change in x

(x_1, y_1)=(-3,1) & (x_2, y_2)= (1,-4)
Slope = [-4 - 1]/[1-(-3)]= -5/4

47. A
The decimal point moves 2 spaces to the left to be placed after 4, which is the first non-zero number. 4.5 x 10^{-2} The exponent is negation since the decimal moved left.

48. D
5575 + 8791 = 14366

49. A

The easiest way to solve age problems is to use a table:

	Mother	Child
Now	7x	x
25 years later	7x + 25	x + 25

Now, mother is 7 times older than her child. So, if we say that the child is x years old, mother is 7x years old. In 25 years, 25 will be added to their ages. We are told that in 25 years, mother's age will double her child's age. So,

$7x + 25 = 2(x + 25)$ ... by solving this equation, we reach x that is the child's age:

$7x + 25 = 2x + 50$

$7x - 2x = 50 - 25$

$5x = 25$

$x = 5$

Mother is 7x years old: $7x = 7 \cdot 5 = 35$

50. C

Let the number be x.

$x/(3/2)$ is the required result.

$x \cdot (3/2)$ is the operation the student does mistakenly. We are told that the multiplication result is 5 more than the division result that is the required one:

$x \cdot (3/2) = x/(3/2) + 5$ ... by solving this equation, we find x.

$3x/2 = 2x/3 + 5$

$3x/2 - 2x/3 = 5$ ... by equating the denominators to 6:

$9x/6 - 4x/6 = 5$

$(9x - 4x)/6 = 5$

$5x/6 = 5$

$5x = 30$

$x = 6$

English Grammar and Usage

1. A
The sentence requires the past perfect "has always been known." This is the only grammatically correct choice.

2. D
When comparing two items, use "the taller." When comparing more than two items, use "the tallest."

3. B
The past perfect form is used to describe an event that occurred in the past and prior to another event. Here there are two things that happened, both of them in the past, and something the person wanted to do.

Event 1: Kiss came to town
Event 2: All the tickets sold out
What I wanted to do: Buy a ticket

The events are arranged:
When KISS came to town, all of the tickets **had been sold out** before I could buy one.

4. A
The subject is "rules" so the present tense plural form, "are," is used to agree with "realize."

5. A
"Who" is correct because the question uses an active construction. "To whom was first place given?" is a passive construction.

6. D
"Which" is correct, because the files are objects and not people.

7. B
The correct sentence is
Historians have been guessing for more than 100 years the doctor was a woman.

Here the phrase 'for more than 100 years' refers to how long historians have been guessing, and not to how long the doctor has been a woman.

8. B
Use a comma separates independent clauses. None of us wants to go to the party, not even if there will be live music.

9. A
This is an example where a comma appears before 'and,' but is disambiguating. Without the comma, the sentence would be "I own two dogs, a cat named Jeffrey and Henry, the goldfish." This means there is a cat named Jeffrey and Henry, and a goldfish with no name mentioned. The comma appears to show the distinction.

I own two dogs, a cat named Jeffrey, and Henry, the goldfish.

10. B
President is not capitalized unless used with a name as in, President Obama.

11. A
The third conditional is used for talking about an unreal situation (a situation that did not happen) in the past. For example, "If I had studied harder, [if clause] I would have passed the exam" [main clause]. This has the same meaning as, "I failed the exam, because I didn't study hard enough."

12. A
Use a plural verb form for two subjects linked by "and."

13. B
In double negative sentences, one of the negatives is replaced with "any."

14. C
"It's" is a contraction for it is or it has. "Its" is a possessive pronoun.

15. A
When two subjects are linked by "with" or "as well," use the verb form that matches the first subject.

Essay Revision

1. D
Suggested revision of sentence 1, "Humankind's thirst for knowledge is insatiable, making curiosity a driving force for advances throughout history."

Use the gender neutral "humankind. Replace the past perfect "has always been" with the present tense to make a simpler and more direct sentence. "Though history" is incorrect. Use "throughout" when referring to a time period. Replace the preposition "for" with "in."

2. A
Sentence 6 is the least relevant. "Curiosity was launched in late November 2011 from Cape Canaveral Air Force Station in Florida."

The third paragraph talks about the objectives of the rover. All sentences other than sentence 6 mention the objectives. This sentence, however, informs about when the spacecraft was launched.

3. D
Suggested changes to sentence 5, "So far, NASA has carried out several exploration missions to Mars and the robot rover "Curiosity" is the latest and most sophisticated of all."

"Curiosity" is the name of a spacecraft that was assigned the particular name because of its association of its mission to satisfy our curiosity about the planet Mars. In this respect, the name bears a special meaning and emphasis which must be reflected in representing it using the quotation mark.

4. D
The changes needed to sentence 5 are, "So far, NASA has carried out several exploratory missions to Mars and the rover robot "Curiosity" is the latest and most sophisticated of all."

"Curiosity" is the name of a spacecraft that was assigned the particular name because of its association of its mission to satisfy our curiosity about the planet Mars. In this respect, the name bears a special meaning and emphasis, which must be reflected in representing it using the quotation mark.

Use of the adjective "exploratory" to describe the missions is correct.

5. C
Sentence 12, which talks about infrared light, is not relevant to the main idea of paragraph 2.

6. C
The correct version of sentence 17 is, "And although the invention is yet to prove its efficiency in harnessing solar energy, a lot of funding has already been dedicated to further research."

Choice C has the correct use of "its" and "a lot."

7. B
Suggested corrections to sentence 10, "Oleic acid, the main ingredient of olive oil, absorbs infra-red radiation, which is the major component of the Sun's radiation reaching the Earth."

The sentence is missing the subordinate conjunction "which" or "that" necessary to construct the subordinate clause, with a comma before "which." Choices B and C suggest these changes, but since choice C contains a punctuation error, only B is has the correct answer.

8. D
Suggested changes to sentence 2, "With continued concern over global climate change, environmentalists are urging governments to lower their dependence on fossil fuels to ensure reduced carbon emission into the atmosphere."

This sentence contains inappropriate use of gerunds and infinitives. To-infinitives are preferred when the continuous form of a main verb is used right before or after them. In this case, "urging" should be followed by the to-infinitive of "lower." Farther in the sentence, the linking phrase "to," has only one acceptable form; itself. Therefore, the verb which is linked to must contain the infinitive form. The gerund form must be discarded. The only valid choice is D.

9. B
Suggested changes to sentence 6 are, "This information, coupled with conventional on-site procedures, help archeologists plan their excavation carefully and efficiently."

The second paragraph points out the significance of satellite imaging for archeological studies. The original sentence only makes a general claim.

10. B
The underlined portion of sentence 6, "coupled with" can be re-written as, "together with."

11. A
The following sentence, inserted after sentence 3, would best illustrate the main idea, "The application has inspired archeologists to use it for searching for the traces of ancient civilizations and other anthropological dynamics."

Choice A points out the significance of the application with some details that are addressed in the subsequent paragraphs. All other choices are either too general, or less relevant to the main idea of the passage.

12. A
Suggested changes to sentence 4 are, "The key feature of the new tool- according to Professor Sarah Parcak, who discovered many cities, temples and pyramids covered under sands and sediment- is that it offers a wider perspective in size and scale of the location."

The changes in this sentence are related to punctuation. The original sentence contains a semicolon before a verbal phrase which is not justifiable with its standard use. The sentence can be modified using parenthetic dashes since using parenthetic commas makes the sentence very complicated as the sentence contains several clauses and a list.

Practice Test Questions Set 2

The questions below are not the same as you will find on the CAHSEE - that would be too easy! And nobody knows what the questions will be and they change all the time. Below are general questions that cover the same subject areas as the CAHSEE. So, while the format and exact wording of the questions may differ slightly, and change from year to year, if you can answer the questions below, you will have no problem with the CAHSEE.

For the best results, take these Practice Test Questions as if it were the real exam. Set aside time when you will not be disturbed, and a location that is quiet and free of distractions. Read the instructions carefully, read each question carefully, and answer to the best of your ability.
Use the bubble answer sheets provided. When you have completed the Practice Questions, check your answer against the Answer Key and read the explanation provided.

Do not attempt more than one set of practice test questions in one day. After completing the first practice test, wait two or three days before attempting the second set of questions.

Reading Answer Sheet

1. Ⓐ Ⓑ Ⓒ Ⓓ 11. Ⓐ Ⓑ Ⓒ Ⓓ 21. Ⓐ Ⓑ Ⓒ Ⓓ
2. Ⓐ Ⓑ Ⓒ Ⓓ 12. Ⓐ Ⓑ Ⓒ Ⓓ 22. Ⓐ Ⓑ Ⓒ Ⓓ
3. Ⓐ Ⓑ Ⓒ Ⓓ 13. Ⓐ Ⓑ Ⓒ Ⓓ 23. Ⓐ Ⓑ Ⓒ Ⓓ
4. Ⓐ Ⓑ Ⓒ Ⓓ 14. Ⓐ Ⓑ Ⓒ Ⓓ 24. Ⓐ Ⓑ Ⓒ Ⓓ
5. Ⓐ Ⓑ Ⓒ Ⓓ 15. Ⓐ Ⓑ Ⓒ Ⓓ 25. Ⓐ Ⓑ Ⓒ Ⓓ
6. Ⓐ Ⓑ Ⓒ Ⓓ 16. Ⓐ Ⓑ Ⓒ Ⓓ 26. Ⓐ Ⓑ Ⓒ Ⓓ
7. Ⓐ Ⓑ Ⓒ Ⓓ 17. Ⓐ Ⓑ Ⓒ Ⓓ 27. Ⓐ Ⓑ Ⓒ Ⓓ
8. Ⓐ Ⓑ Ⓒ Ⓓ 18. Ⓐ Ⓑ Ⓒ Ⓓ 28. Ⓐ Ⓑ Ⓒ Ⓓ
9. Ⓐ Ⓑ Ⓒ Ⓓ 19. Ⓐ Ⓑ Ⓒ Ⓓ 29. Ⓐ Ⓑ Ⓒ Ⓓ
10. Ⓐ Ⓑ Ⓒ Ⓓ 20. Ⓐ Ⓑ Ⓒ Ⓓ 30. Ⓐ Ⓑ Ⓒ Ⓓ

Mathematics Answer Sheet

1. A B C D
2. A B C D
3. A B C D
4. A B C D
5. A B C D
6. A B C D
7. A B C D
8. A B C D
9. A B C D
10. A B C D
11. A B C D
12. A B C D
13. A B C D
14. A B C D
15. A B C D
16. A B C D
17. A B C D
18. A B C D
19. A B C D
20. A B C D
21. A B C D
22. A B C D
23. A B C D
24. A B C D
25. A B C D
26. A B C D
27. A B C D
28. A B C D
29. A B C D
30. A B C D
31. A B C D
32. A B C D
33. A B C D
34. A B C D
35. A B C D
36. A B C D
37. A B C D
38. A B C D
39. A B C D
40. A B C D
41. A B C D
42. A B C D
43. A B C D
44. A B C D
45. A B C D
46. A B C D
47. A B C D
48. A B C D
49. A B C D
50. A B C D

Essay Revision - English Grammar and Usage Answer Sheet

1. Ⓐ Ⓑ Ⓒ Ⓓ 11. Ⓐ Ⓑ Ⓒ Ⓓ 21. Ⓐ Ⓑ Ⓒ Ⓓ
2. Ⓐ Ⓑ Ⓒ Ⓓ 12. Ⓐ Ⓑ Ⓒ Ⓓ 22. Ⓐ Ⓑ Ⓒ Ⓓ
3. Ⓐ Ⓑ Ⓒ Ⓓ 13. Ⓐ Ⓑ Ⓒ Ⓓ 23. Ⓐ Ⓑ Ⓒ Ⓓ
4. Ⓐ Ⓑ Ⓒ Ⓓ 14. Ⓐ Ⓑ Ⓒ Ⓓ 24. Ⓐ Ⓑ Ⓒ Ⓓ
5. Ⓐ Ⓑ Ⓒ Ⓓ 15. Ⓐ Ⓑ Ⓒ Ⓓ 25. Ⓐ Ⓑ Ⓒ Ⓓ
6. Ⓐ Ⓑ Ⓒ Ⓓ 16. Ⓐ Ⓑ Ⓒ Ⓓ 26. Ⓐ Ⓑ Ⓒ Ⓓ
7. Ⓐ Ⓑ Ⓒ Ⓓ 17. Ⓐ Ⓑ Ⓒ Ⓓ 27. Ⓐ Ⓑ Ⓒ Ⓓ
8. Ⓐ Ⓑ Ⓒ Ⓓ 18. Ⓐ Ⓑ Ⓒ Ⓓ 28. Ⓐ Ⓑ Ⓒ Ⓓ
9. Ⓐ Ⓑ Ⓒ Ⓓ 19. Ⓐ Ⓑ Ⓒ Ⓓ 29. Ⓐ Ⓑ Ⓒ Ⓓ
10. Ⓐ Ⓑ Ⓒ Ⓓ 20. Ⓐ Ⓑ Ⓒ Ⓓ 30. Ⓐ Ⓑ Ⓒ Ⓓ

Part 1 – Reading and Language Arts

Questions 1-4 refer to the following passage.

The Respiratory System

The respiratory system's function is to allow oxygen exchange through all parts of the body. The anatomy or structure of the exchange system, and the uses of the exchanged gases, varies depending on the organism. In humans and other mammals, for example, the anatomical features of the respiratory system include airways, lungs, and the respiratory muscles. Molecules of oxygen and carbon dioxide are passively exchanged, by diffusion, between the gaseous external environment and the blood. This exchange process occurs in the alveolar region of the lungs.

Other animals, such as insects, have respiratory systems with very simple anatomical features, and in amphibians even the skin plays a vital role in gas exchange. Plants also have respiratory systems but the direction of gas exchange can be opposite to that of animals.

The respiratory system can also be divided into physiological, or functional, zones. These include the conducting zone (the region for gas transport from the outside atmosphere to just above the alveoli), the transitional zone, and the respiratory zone (the alveolar region where gas exchange occurs). [8]

1. What can we infer from the first paragraph in this passage?

    a. Human and mammal respiratory systems are the same

    b. The lungs are an important part of the respiratory system

    c. The respiratory system varies in different mammals

    d. Oxygen and carbon dioxide are passive exchanged by the respiratory system

2. What is the process by which molecules of oxygen and carbon dioxide are passively exchanged?

    a. Transfusion
    b. Affusion
    c. Diffusion
    d. Respiratory confusion

3. What organ plays an important role in gas exchange in amphibians?

    a. The skin
    b. The lungs
    c. The gills
    d. The mouth

4. What are the three physiological zones of the respiratory system?

    a. Conducting, transitional, respiratory zones
    b. Redacting, transitional, circulatory zones
    c. Conducting, circulatory, inhibiting zones
    d. Transitional, inhibiting, conducting zones

Questions 5-8 refer to the following passage.

ABC Electric Warranty

ABC Electric Company warrants that its products are free from defects in material and workmanship. Subject to the conditions and limitations set forth below, ABC Electric will, at its option, either repair or replace any part of its products that prove defective due to improper workmanship or materials.

This limited warranty does not cover any damage to the product from improper installation, accident, abuse, misuse, natural disaster, insufficient or excessive electrical supply, abnormal mechanical or environmental conditions, or any unauthorized disassembly, repair, or modification.

This limited warranty also does not apply to any product on which the original identification information has been altered, or removed, has not been handled or packaged correctly, or has been sold as second-hand.

This limited warranty covers only repair, replacement, refund or credit for defective ABC Electric products, as provided above.

5. I tried to repair my ABC Electric blender, but could not, so can I get it repaired under this warranty?

    a. Yes, the warranty still covers the blender

    b. No, the warranty does not cover the blender

    c. Uncertain. ABC Electric may or may not cover repairs under this warranty

6. My ABC Electric fan is not working. Will ABC Electric provide a new one or repair this one?

    a. ABC Electric will repair my fan

    b. ABC Electric will replace my fan

    c. ABC Electric could either replace or repair my fan or I can request either a replacement or a repair.

7. My stove was damaged in a flood. Does this warranty cover my stove?

    a. Yes, it is covered.

    b. No, it is not covered.

    c. It may or may not be covered.

    d. ABC Electric will decide if it is covered

8. Which of the following is an example of improper workmanship?

    a. Missing parts
    b. Defective parts
    c. Scratches on the front
    d. None of the above

Questions 9 - 12 refer to the following passage.

Low Blood Sugar

As the name suggest, low blood sugar is low sugar levels in the bloodstream. This can occur when you have not eaten properly and undertake strenuous activity, or when you are very hungry. When Low blood sugar occurs regularly and is ongoing, it is a medical condition called hypoglycemia. This condition can occur in diabetics and also in healthy adults.

Causes of low blood sugar can include excessive alcohol consumption, metabolic problems, stomach surgery, pancreas, liver or kidneys problems, as well as a side-effect of some medications.

Symptoms

There are different symptoms depending on the severity of the case.

Mild hypoglycemia can lead to feelings of nausea and hunger. The patient may also feel nervous, jittery and have fast heart beats. Sweaty skin, clammy and cold skin are likely symptoms.

Moderate hypoglycemia can result in a short temper, confusion, nervousness, fear and blurring of vision. The patient may feel weak and unsteady.

Severe cases of hypoglycemia can lead to seizures, coma, fainting spells, nightmares, headaches, excessive sweats and severe tiredness.

Diagnosis of low blood sugar

A doctor can diagnosis this medical condition by asking the patient questions and testing blood and urine samples. Home testing kits are available for patients to monitor blood sugar levels. It is important to see a qualified doctor though. The doctor can administer tests to ensure that will safely rule out other medical conditions that could affect blood sugar levels.

Treatment

Quick treatments include drinking or eating foods and drinks with high sugar contents. Good examples include soda, fruit juice, hard candy and raisins. Glucose energy tablets can also help. Doctors may also recommend medications and well as changes in diet and exercise routine to treat chronic low blood sugar.

9. Based on the article, which of the following is true?

    a. Low blood sugar can happen to anyone.

    b. Low blood sugar only happens to diabetics.

    c. Low blood sugar can occur even.

    d. None of the statements are true.

10. Which of the following are the author's opinion?

    a. Quick treatments include drinking or eating foods and drinks with high sugar contents.

    b. None of the statements are opinions.

    c. This condition can occur in diabetics and also in healthy adults.

    d. There are different symptoms depending on the severity of the case

11. What is the author's purpose?

a. To inform

b. To persuade

c. To entertain

d. To analyze

12. Which of the following is not a detail?

a. A doctor can diagnosis this medical condition by asking the patient questions and testing.

b. A doctor will test blood and urine samples.

c. Glucose energy tablets can also help.

d. Home test kits monitor blood sugar levels.

Chapter 1 - Getting Started

A Better Score Is Possible 6
Types of Multiple Choice 9
Multiple Choice Step-by-Step 12
Tips for Reading the Instructions 13
General Multiple Choice Tips 14
Multiple Choice Strategy Practice 20
Answer Key 39

13. Based on the partial Table of Contents above, what is this book about?

a. How to answer multiple choice questions

b. Different types of multiple choice questions

c. How to write a test

d. None of the above

Questions 14-17 refer to the following passage.

Myths, Legend and Folklore

Cultural historians draw a distinction between myth, legend and folktale simply as a way to group traditional stories. However, in many cultures, drawing a sharp line between myths and legends is not that simple. Instead of dividing their traditional stories into myths, legends, and folktales, some cultures divide them into two categories. The first category roughly corresponds to folktales, and the second is one that combines myths and legends. Similarly, we can not always separate myths from folktales. One society might consider a story true, making it a myth. Another society may believe the story is fiction, which makes it a folktale. In fact, when a myth loses its status as part of a religious system, it often takes on traits more typical of folktales, with its formerly divine characters now appearing as human heroes, giants, or fairies. Myth, legend, and folktale are only a few of the categories of traditional stories. Other categories include anecdotes and some kinds of jokes. Traditional stories, in turn, are only one category within the larger category of folklore, which also includes items such as gestures, costumes, and music. [9]

14. The main idea of this passage is that

    a. Myths, fables, and folktales are not the same thing, and each describes a specific type of story

    b. Traditional stories can be categorized in different ways by different people

    c. Cultures use myths for religious purposes, and when this is no longer true, the people forget and discard these myths

    d. Myths can never become folk tales, because one is true, and the other is false

15. The terms myth and legend are

   a. Categories that are synonymous with true and false

   b. Categories that group traditional stories according to certain characteristics

   c. Interchangeable, because both terms mean a story that is passed down from generation to generation

   d. Meant to distinguish between a story that involves a hero and a cultural message and a story meant only to entertain

16. Traditional story categories not only include myths and legends, but

   a. Can also include gestures, since some cultures passed these down before the written and spoken word

   b. In addition, folklore refers to stories involving fables and fairy tales

   c. These story categories can also include folk music and traditional dress

   d. Traditional stories themselves are a part of the larger category of folklore, which may also include costumes, gestures, and music

17. This passage shows that

   a. There is a distinct difference between a myth and a legend, although both are folktales

   b. Myths are folktales, but folktales are not myths

   c. Myths, legends, and folktales play an important part in tradition and the past, and are a rich and colorful part of history

   d. Most cultures consider myths to be true

Questions 18 - 20 refer to the following passage.

Lowest Price Guarantee

Get it for less. Guaranteed!

ABC Electric will beat any advertised price by 10% of the difference.

> 1) If you find a lower advertised price, we will beat it by 10% of the difference.
>
> 2) If you find a lower advertised price within 30 days* of your purchase we will beat it by 10% of the difference.
>
> 3) If our own price is reduced within 30 days* of your purchase, bring in your receipt and we will refund the difference.

*14 days for computers, monitors, printers, laptops, tablets, cellular & wireless devices, home security products, projectors, camcorders, digital cameras, radar detectors, portable DVD players, DJ and pro-audio equipment, and air conditioners.

18. I bought a radar detector 15 days ago and saw an ad for the same model only cheaper. Can I get 10% of the difference refunded?

> a. Yes. Since it is less than 30 days, you can get 10% of the difference refunded.
>
> b. No. Since it is more than 14 days, you cannot get 10% of the difference re-funded.
>
> c. It depends on the cashier.
>
> d. Yes. You can get the difference refunded.

19. I bought a flat-screen TV for $500 10 days ago and found an advertisement for the same TV, at another store, on sale for $400. How much will ABC refund under this guarantee?

    a. $100
    b. $110
    c. $10
    d. $400

20. What is the purpose of this passage?

    a. To inform
    b. To educate
    c. To persuade
    d. To entertain

Questions 21 - 23 refer to the following passage.

Insects

Insects have segmented bodies supported by an exoskeleton, a hard outer covering made mostly of chitin. The segments of the body are organized into three distinctive connected units, a head, a thorax, and an abdomen. The head supports a pair of antennae, a pair of compound eyes, and three sets of appendages that form the mouthparts.

The thorax has six segmented legs and, if present in the species, two or four wings. The abdomen consists of eleven segments, though in a few species these segments may be fused together or very small.

Overall, there are 24 segments. The abdomen also contains most of the digestive, respiratory, excretory and reproductive internal structures. There is considerable variation and many adaptations in the body parts of insects especially wings, legs, antenna and mouthparts. [10]

21. How many units do insects have?

    a. Insects are divided into 24 units.

    b. Insects are divided into 3 units.

    c. Insects are divided into segments not units.

    d. It depends on the species.

22. Which of the following is true?

    a. All insects have 2 wings.

    b. All insects have 4 wings.

    c. Some insects have 2 wings.

    d. Some insects have 2 or 4 wings.

23. What is true of insect's abdomen?

    a. It contains some of the organs.

    b. It is too small for any organs.

    c. It contains all of the organs.

    d. None of the above.

Questions 24 - 27 refer to the following passage.

The Daffodils
by William Wordsworth

I wandered lonely as a cloud
That floats on high o'er vales and hills,
When all at once I saw a crowd,
A host, of golden daffodils;
Beside the lake, beneath the trees,
Fluttering and dancing in the breeze.

Continuous as the stars that shine
And twinkle on the Milky Way,
They stretched in never-ending line
Along the margin of a bay:

Ten thousand saw I at a glance,
Tossing their heads in sprightly dance.

The waves beside them danced, but they
Out-did the sparkling waves in glee:
A Poet could not but be gay,
In such a jocund company:
I gazed--and gazed--but little thought
What wealth the show to me had brought:

For oft, when on my couch I lie
In vacant or in pensive mood,
They flash upon that inward eye
Which is the bliss of solitude;
And then my heart with pleasure fills,
And dances with the daffodils.

24. Is the author of this poem a lover of nature?

    a. Yes

    b. No

    c. Uncertain. There isn't enough information

25. What is the general mood of this poem?

    a. Sad

    b. Thoughtful

    c. Happy

    d. Excited

26. What does sprightly mean?

    a. Growing very fast

    b. Sad and melancholy

    c. Weak and slow

    d. Happy and full of life

27. What is jocund company?

    a. Sad
    b. Happy
    c. Joyful
    d. Boring

Questions 28 - 30 refer to the following passage.

Blood

Blood is a specialized bodily fluid that delivers nutrients and oxygen to the body's cells and transports waste products away.

In vertebrates, blood consists of blood cells suspended in a liquid called blood plasma. Plasma, which comprises 55% of blood fluid, is mostly water (90% by volume), and contains dissolved proteins, glucose, mineral ions, hormones, carbon dioxide, platelets and the blood cells themselves.

Blood cells are mainly red blood cells (also called RBCs or erythrocytes) and white blood cells, including leukocytes and platelets. Red blood cells are the most abundant cells, and contain an iron-containing protein called hemoglobin that transports oxygen through the body.

The pumping action of the heart circulates blood around the body through blood vessels. In animals with lungs, arterial blood carries oxygen from inhaled air to the tissues of the body, and venous blood carries carbon dioxide, a waste product of metabolism produced by cells, from the tissues to the lungs to be exhaled. [11]

28. What can we infer from the first paragraph in this passage?

   a. Blood is responsible for transporting oxygen to the cells.

   b. Blood is only red when it reaches the outside of the body.

   c. Each person has about six pints of blood.

   d. Blood's true function was only learned in the last century.

29. Which of these is not contained in blood plasma?

   a. Hormones
   b. Mineral ions
   c. Calcium
   d. Glucose

30. Which body part exhales carbon dioxide after venous blood has carried it from body tissues?

   a. The lungs
   b. The skin cells
   c. The bowels
   d. The sweat glands

Mathematics

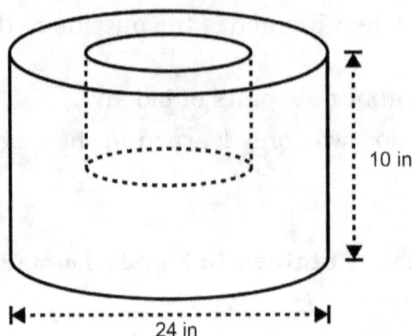

Note: figure not drawn to scale

1. What is the volume of the above solid made by a hollow cylinder that is half the size (in all dimensions) of the larger cylinder?

    a. 1440 π in³

    b. 1260 π in³

    c. 1040 π in³

    d. 960 π in³

2. Driver B drove his car 20 km/h faster than the driver A, and driver B travelled 480 km 2 hours before driver A. What was the speed of driver A?

    a. 70

    b. 80

    c. 60

    d. 90

3. If a train travels at 72 kilometers per hour, how far will it travel in 12 seconds?

    a. 200 meters
    b. 220 meters
    c. 240 meters
    d. 260 meters

4. Tony bought 15 dozen eggs for $80. 16 eggs were broken during loading and unloading. He sold the remaining eggs for $0.54 each. What will be his percent profit?

    a. 11%
    b. 11.2%
    c. 11.5%
    d. 12%

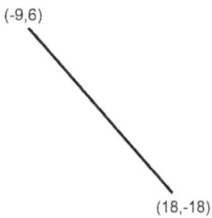

5. What is the slope of the line above?

    a. -8/9
    b. 9/8
    c. -9/8
    d. 8/9

6. Using the quadratic formula, solve the quadratic equation:

$$\frac{x+2}{x-2} + \frac{x-2}{x+2} = 0$$

    a. It has infinite numbers of solutions
    b. 0 and 1
    c. It has no solutions
    d. 0

7. Turn the following expression into a simple polynomial:

$5(3x^2 - 2) - x^2(2 - 3x)$

    a. $3x^3 + 17x^2 - 10$
    b. $3x^3 + 13x^2 + 10$
    c. $-3x^3 - 13x^2 - 10$
    d. $3x^3 + 13x^2 - 10$

8. In a class of 83 students, 72 are present. What percent of students are absent?

    a. 12%
    b. 13%
    c. 14%
    d. 15%

9. Solve $(x^3 + 2)(x^2 - x) - x^5$.

    a. $2x^5 - x^4 + 2x^2 - 2x$
    b. $-x^4 + 2x^2 - 2x$
    c. $-x^4 - 2x^2 - 2x$
    d. $-x^4 + 2x^2 + 2x$

10. $9ab^2 + 8ab^2 =$

   a. ab^2
   b. $17ab^2$
   c. 17
   d. $17a^2b^2$

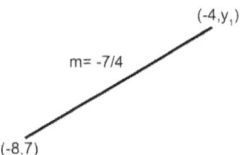

11. With the data given above, what is the value of y_1?

   a. 0
   b. -7
   c. 7
   d. 8

12. Using the factoring method, solve the quadratic equation: $x^2 + 12x - 13 = 0$

   a. -13 and 1
   b. -13 and -1
   c. 1 and 13
   d. -1 and 13

13. In a local election at polling station A, 945 voters cast their vote out of 1270 registered voters. At polling station B, 860 cast their vote out of 1050 registered voters and at station C, 1210 cast their vote out of 1440 registered voters. What was the total turnout including all three polling stations?

    a. 70%

    b. 74%

    c. 76%

    d. 80%

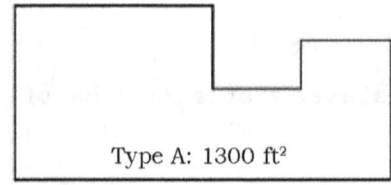

Type A: 1300 ft²

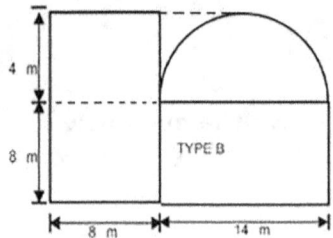

14. The price of houses in a certain subdivision is based on the total area. Susan is watching her budget and wants to choose the house with the lowest area. Which house type, A (1300 ft²) or B, should she choose if she would like the house with the lowest price?
(1cm² = 4.0ft² & π = 22/7)

    a. Type B is smaller 140 ft²

    b. Type A is smaller

    c. Type B is smaller at 855 ft²

    d. Type B is larger

15. Find the mean of these set of numbers: 1, 2, 3, 4, 5, 6, 7, 8, 9, 10.

   a. 55
   b. 5.5
   c. 11
   d. 10

16. If a and b are real numbers, solve the following equation: $(a + 2)x - b = -2 + (a + b)x$

   a. -1
   b. 0
   c. 1
   d. 2

17. The area of a rectangle is 20 cm². If one side increases by 1 cm and other by 2 cm, the area of the new rectangle is 35 cm². Find the sides of the original rectangle.

   a. (4,8)
   b. (4,5)
   c. (2.5,8)
   d. b and c

18. Below are the number of people that attended a particular church every Friday for 7 weeks. Find the mean. 62, 18, 39, 13, 16, 37, 25.

   a. 25
   b. 210
   c. 62
   d. 30

19. Consider the following graph.

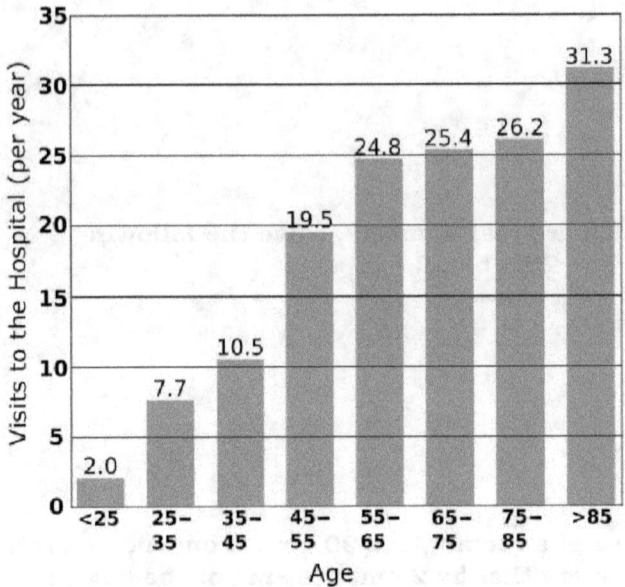

How many hospital visits per year does a person aged 85 or more make?

   a. 26.2
   b. 31.3
   c. More than 31.3
   d. A decision cannot be made from this graph.

20. Based on this graph, how many visits per year do you expect a person that is 95 or older to make?

   a. More than 31.3
   b. Less than 31.3
   c. 31.3
   d. A decision cannot be made from this graph.

21. How much water can be stored in a cylindrical container 5 meters in diameter and 12 meters high?

Note: figure not drawn to scale

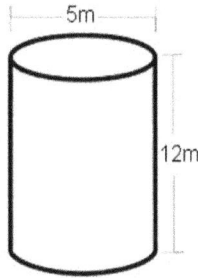

a. 235.65 m³
b. 223.65 m³
c. 240.65 m³
d. 252.65 m³

22. Find the solution for the following linear equation: 1/4 x - 2 = 5/6

a. 0.2
b. 0.4
c. 0.6
d. 0.8

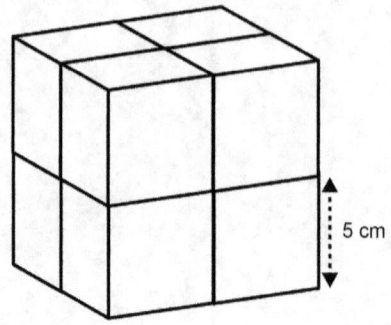

Note: figure not drawn to scale

23. Assuming the figure is composed of cubes, what is the volume of the figure above?

    a. 125 cm³

    b. 875 cm³

    c. 1000 cm³

    d. 500 cm³

24. Choose the expression the figure represents.

    a. X > 2

    b. X ≥ 2

    c. X < 2

    d. X ≤ 2

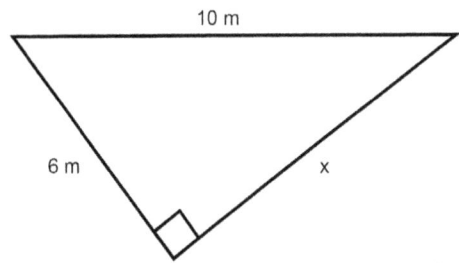

25. What is the length of the missing side in the triangle above?

    a. 6
    b. 4
    c. 8
    d. 5

26. Solve
$x \sqrt{5} - y = \sqrt{5}$
$x - y \sqrt{5} = 5$

    a. $(0, -\sqrt{5})$
    b. $(0, \sqrt{5})$
    c. $(-\sqrt{5}, 0)$
    d. $(\sqrt{5}, 0)$

27. If $A = -2x^4 + x^2 - 3x$, $B = x^4 - x^3 + 5$ and $C = x^4 + 2x^3 + 4x + 5$, find $A + B - C$.

    a. $x^3 + x^2 + x + 10$
    b. $-3x^3 + x^2 - 7x + 10$
    c. $-2x^4 - 3x^3 + x^2 - 7x$
    d. $-3x^4 + x^3 + x^2 - 7x$

**28. Find the median of this set of numbers:
1,2,3,4,5,6,7,8,9 and 10**

    a. 55
    b. 10
    c. 1
    d. 5.5

29. Convert 0.00002011 to scientific notation

    a. 2.011×10^{-4}
    b. 2.011×10^{5}
    c. 2.011×10^{-6}
    d. 2.011×10^{-5}

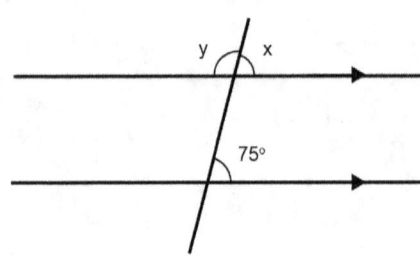

30. What is the value of the angle y?

    a. 25°
    b. 15°
    c. 30°
    d. 105°

31. Find the square of 25/9

    a. 5/3
    b. 3/5
    c. 7 58/81
    d. 15/2

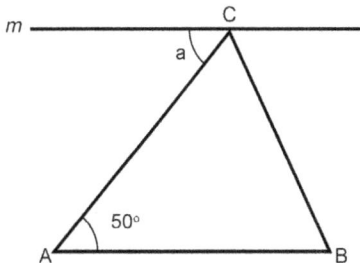

32. If the line *m* is parallel to the side AB of △ABC, what is angle *a*?

    a. 130°
    b. 25°
    c. 65°
    d. 50°

33. Find the median of this set of numbers: 100, 200, 450, 29, 1029, 300 and 2001

    a. 300
    b. 29
    c. 7
    d. 4,080

34. Which one of the following is less than a third?

    a. 84/231
    b. 6/35
    c. 3/22
    d. b and c

35. Which of the following numbers is the largest?

   a. 1
   b. $\sqrt{2}$
   c. 3/2
   d. 4/3

36. $(4Y^3 - 2Y^2) + (7Y^2 + 3y - y) =$

   a. $4y^3 + 9y^2 + 4y$
   b. $5y^3 + 5y^2 + 3y$
   c. $4y^3 + 7y^2 + 2y$
   d. $4y^3 + 5y^2 + 2y$

37. $7(2y + 8) + 1 - 4(y + 5) =$

   a. $10y + 36$
   b. $10y + 77$
   c. $18y + 37$
   d. $10y + 37$

(18,12)

(9,-6)

38. What is the distance between the two points?

   a. ≈19
   b. 20
   c. ≈21
   d. ≈22

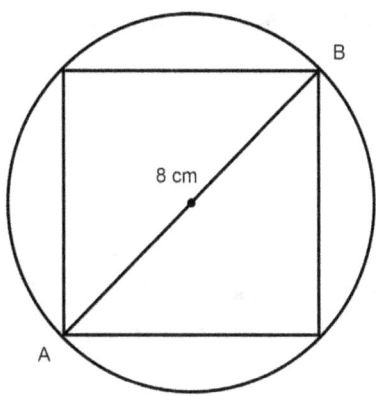

Note: figure not drawn to scale

39. What is area of the circle?

    a. 4π cm²
    b. 12π cm²
    c. 10π cm²
    d. 16π cm²

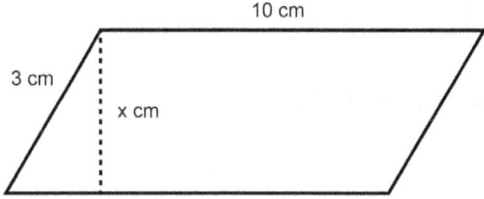

40. What is the perimeter of the parallelogram above?

    a. 12 cm
    b. 26 cm
    c. 13 cm
    d. (13+x) cm

41. Richard gives 's' amount of salary to each of his 'n' employees weekly. If he has 'x' amount of money then how many days he can employ these 'n' employees.

    a. sx/7n
    b. 7x/nx
    c. nx/7s
    d. 7x/ns

42. Find the mode from these test results: 17, 19, 18, 17, 18, 19, 11, 17, 16, 19, 15, 15, 15, 17, 13, 11

    a. 15
    b. 11
    c. 17
    d. 19

43. A map uses a scale of 1:100,000. How much distance on the ground is 3 inches on the map if the scale is in inches?

    a. 13 inches
    b. 300,000 inches
    c. 30,000 inches
    d. 333.999 inches

44. Subtract 456,890 from 465,890.

    a. 9,000
    b. 7000
    c. 8970
    d. 8500

45. Susan wants to buy a leather jacket that costs $545.00 and is on sale for 10% off. What is the approximate cost?

    a. $525
    b. $450
    c. $475
    d. $500

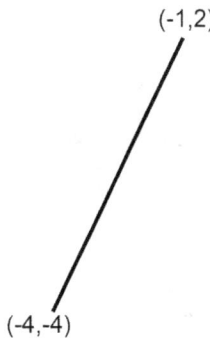

46. What is the slope of the line above?

    a. 1
    b. 2
    c. 3
    d. -2

47. Convert 204 to scientific notation.

    a. 2.04×10^{-2}
    b. 0.204×10^{2}
    c. 2.04×10^{3}
    d. 2.04×10^{2}

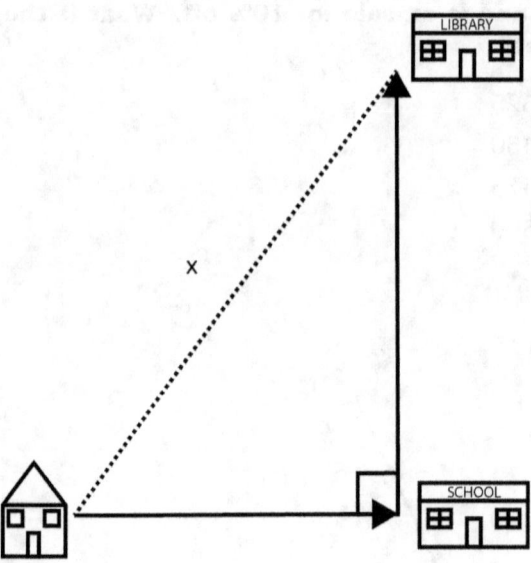

48. Every day starting from his home Peter travels due east 3 kilometers to the school. After school he travels due north 4 kilometers to the library. What is the distance between Peter's home and the library?

    a. 15 km
    b. 10 km
    c. 5 km
    d. 12 ½ km

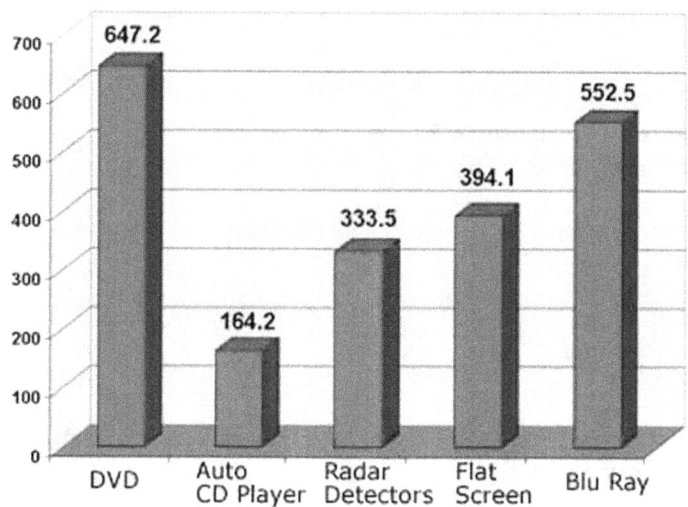

49. Consider the graph above. What is the third best-selling product?

    a. Radar Detectors
    b. Flat Screen
    c. Blu Ray
    d. Auto CD Players

50. Which two products are the closest in the number of sales?

    a. Blu Ray and Flat Screen TV
    b. Flat Screen TV and Radar Detectors
    c. Radar Detectors and Auto CD Players
    d. DVD players and Blu Ray

English Grammar and Usage

1. Elaine promised to bring the camera _____ at the mall yesterday.

    a. by me
    b. with me
    c. at me
    d. to me

2. Last night, he _____ the sleeping bag down beside my mattress.

    a. lay
    b. laid
    c. lain
    d. has laid

3. I would have bought the shirt for you if

    a. I had known you liked it.
    b. I have known you liked it.
    c. I would know you liked it.
    d. I know you liked it.

4. Many believers still hope _____ proof of the existence of ghosts.

    a. two find
    b. to find
    c. to found
    d. to have been found

Practice Test Questions 2

5. Choose the sentence with the correct grammar.

   a. The court summons was placed on his desk
   b. The court summons are placed on his desk
   c. The court summons were placed on his desk
   d. None of the above

6. If he _____ the textbook like he was supposed to, he would have known what was on the test.

   a. will have read
   b. shouldn't have read
   c. would have read
   d. had read

7. Following the tornado, telephone poles _____ all over the street.

   a. laid
   b. lied
   c. were lying
   d. were laying

8. Choose the sentence with the correct grammar.

   a. Neither the teacher nor the students is left in class.
   b. Neither the teacher nor the students was left in class.
   c. Neither the teacher nor the students are left in class.
   d. None of the above.

9. After the car was fixed, it _____ again.

   a. ran good
   b. ran well
   c. would have run well
   d. ran more well

10. Choose the correct sentence.

a. Their only employee with a nose ring is a young man named Daniel.

b. Their only employee is a young man named Daniel with a nose ring.

c. Their only employee is a young man with a nose ring named Daniel.

d. A and C are correct.

11. Choose the sentence with the correct grammar.

a. Everyone are to wear a black tie.

b. Everyone have to wear a black tie.

c. Everyone has to wear a black tie.

d. None of the above.

12. Choose the sentence with the correct grammar.

a. The salmon has been cooked.

b. The salmon have been cooked.

c. Both of the above.

d. None of the above.

13. The Ford Motor Company was named for Henry Ford, _____.

a. which had founded the company.

b. who founded the company.

c. whose had founded the company.

d. whom had founded the company.

14. The weatherman on Channel 6 said that this has been the _____.

   a. most hotter summer on record

   b. most hottest summer on record

   c. hottest summer on record

   d. hotter summer on record

15. As the tallest monument in the United States, the St. Louis Arch _____.

   a. has rose to an impressive 630 feet.

   b. is risen to an impressive 630 feet.

   c. rises to an impressive 630 feet.

   d. was rose to an impressive 630 feet.

Essay Revision

Abuse of Science: The Atom Bomb

The cost of the two World Wars – not to mention the lives lost – could have easily paid for the entire energy consumption of the nations which waged them. [1] Even today, world powers are spending hundreds of billions of dollars sponsoring wars in a bid to control oil-rich areas. [2] Spending such astronomic sums on peaceful, environment friendly sources of energy would certainly produce results that would limit the energy needs of the planet as a whole. [3] Not to mention, resolving the conflicts between warring nations. [4]

For instance the atom bomb was developed during the Second World War by the recommendations of the great Albert Einstein - who is accepted as the father of modern physics; in fear of the Germans developing it and using on the Allies. [5] No matter what, the technology behind the atom bomb had the power to resolve the war. [6] Using it to produce energy for power was an option wide open to be explored by scientists. [7] Today, as many as forty countries including countries like Egypt, harness nuclear energy as a dominant source of power alongside mainstream carbon sources. [8]

The two atom bombs dropped at Hiroshima and Nagasaki, as the consequence of the tragedy at Pearl Harbor, left catastrophic legacies to the generations that followed. [9] The generations that followed still have not recovered from the genetic disorders. [10] Almost seven decades passing later, abnormal births and birth defects continue to occur. [11]

1. Which sentence from the passage is an example of a sentence fragment?

    a. 3

    b. 4

    c. 5

    d. 6

2. Which of the following changes would focus attention on the main idea of the second paragraph?

    a. Yet, the technology behind the atom bomb essentially had the power of resolving the war itself which scientists like him failed to convey.

    b. As a result of that, the technology behind the atom bomb essentially had the power of resolving the war itself which scientists like him failed to convey.

    c. With respect to that, the technology behind the atom bomb essentially had the power of resolving the war itself which scientists like him failed to convey.

    d. Additionally, the technology behind the atom bomb essentially had the power of resolving the war itself which scientists like him failed to convey.

3. Which of the following changes are needed in sentence 5?

a. For instance the atom bomb was developed during the Second World War by the recommendations of the great Albert Einstein - who is accepted as the father of modern physics - in fear of the Germans developing it and using on the Allies.

b. For example, the atom bomb was developed during the Second World War by the recommendations of the great Albert Einstein - who is accepted as the father of modern physics - in fear of the Germans developing it and using on the Allies.

c. For instance, the atom bomb was developed during the Second World War by the recommendations of the great Albert Einstein; who is accepted as the father of modern physics - in fear of the Germans developing it and using on the Allies.

d. For instance, the atom bomb was developed during the Second World War by the recommendations of the great Albert Einstein; who is accepted as the father of modern physics, in fear of the Germans developing it and using on the Allies.

4. Which of the following sentences, if inserted before sentence 7, would best illustrate the main idea of the passage?

a. The name of the technology is widely referred to in current science books published worldwide as nuclear fission.

b. This technology is, however, misused by many irresponsible states in the world today.

c. Nuclear fission that is used in the fuelling of the bomb, has the capacity to produce electrical energy which has turned out to be a major alternative later in the Twentieth Century.

d. Nuclear fission, which is the main technology behind the development of the atom bomb can also be used to produce gamma rays which has many applications in medical science.

Leg Surgery

The main reason many young women opt for surgery, despite the pain, inconvenience and cost, is the height discrimination in an increasingly competitive job market. [1] Almost all firms put certain height criteria for the candidates who apply. [2] For example, for an air stewardess position, women must be no more than 163 cm tall; whereas for jobs in foreign affairs, Chinese diplomats are required to match their foreign counterparts. [3] Height concerns also effect routine citizenship privileges such as driving licenses, which require a height of at least 157 cm to be eligible for taking the test in some places. [4]

The urge to undergo surgery is becoming increasingly popular among Chinese males as well. [5] "It offers me a 10 cm increase in my height, which can dramatically change my future," says Jing Yong, an interpreter working in Hong Kong. [6] "This will allow me better opportunities in the competitive job market here," adds the young multilingual who couldn't make it to the foreign ministry for being below 168 cm. [7] Even parents approve of the idea, being fully aware of all the complexity and they are willing to finance such a labyrinth surgery. [8] "It's something that will give her confidence and achieve her goals in life. [9] Her height used to bother her tremendously, now this can change that," comments Swee Jing's father by her bedside as she is recovering from the eighteen-months process that involves elongating her tibia and fibula by placing two rods that will stimulate the extra growth of the bones. [10] They too are hopeful about the possibilities the surgery would affect the life of their daughter. [11]

5. Which sentence in the first paragraph is least relevant to the main idea of the first paragraph?

    a. 2
    b. 3
    c. 4
    d. 5

6. Which sentence is not consistent with the author's purpose?

    a. 3

    b. 6

    c. 9

    d. 12

7. Which of the following sentences, if inserted after sentence 7, would best illustrate the main idea of the passage?

    a. This is the main reason I am willing to undergo this surgery

    b. This artificial way of gaining height is turning out to be a new trend among the new generation in height conscious China.

    c. Height is a very big problem for Chinese people, particularly for those who wish to go abroad and carry the flag of China there.

    d. Young people like Yong will have to spend the rest of their lives with a fake pair of legs though.

8. Which of the following changes are needed in sentence 8?

    a. Even parents approve of the idea, being fully aware of all the sophistications and they are willing to finance such a labyrinth surgery.

    b. Even parents approve of the idea, being fully aware of all the complications and they are willing to finance such a sophisticated surgery.

    c. Even parents approve of the idea, being fully aware of all the complexity and they are willing to finance such a sophisticated surgery.

    d. Even parents approve of the idea, being fully aware of all the complexity and they are willing to finance such a sophisticated surgery.

My Friend Luke

My forty-year old friend Luke is possibly the sweetest, shyest person enjoying his life on the entire Earth. [1] He is somewhat short, skinny and upright; has a thin moustache and a thinner trace of hair covering his head. [2] And since he has problems seeing distant things, he wears glasses that are small, thick and frameless; the round coffee-brown colored glasses give him a cool appearance uniquely suited to his personality. [3] Which I doubt belongs to any other person other than him. [4]

There are traits in him seldom found in others. [5] While in a crowd, he walks sideways so as not to trouble others. [6] Instead of requesting a space to move ahead, he glides past to one side of the person blocking in his way. [7] If the gap turns out to be so narrow that it does not permit his bony frame to pass, he waits patiently for the person to move out of the way. [8] He is panicked by street dogs and neighbors' cats and to avoid them, he crosses to the other side of the street every now and then. [9]

Luke never speaks, as he thinks speaking is a waste of energy; something he is vehemently dedicated to saving. [10] Whenever he does, in order not to interrupt anybody, he speaks with a very soft, low tone – in a way no one ever notices him speaking in the first place. [11] Quite ironically, when he gets a rare chance to speak, he never succeeds in speaking more than two words before being interrupted by others. [12]

9. What sentence from the passage is an example of a sentence fragment?

    a. 4
    b. 5
    c. 6
    d. 7

10. Which sentence in the second paragraph is least relevant to the main idea of the second paragraph?

   a. 6
   b. 7
   c. 8
   d. 9

11. Which of the following sentences should be modified to reduce redundancy?

   a. 2
   b. 3
   c. 4
   d. 5

12. Which of the following sentences, if inserted before sentence 1, would best illustrate the main idea of the passage?

   a. But that does not bother him; rather he always seems to be happy in being able to utter those two words.

   b. Interestingly, he never insists in speaking with people more eloquently.

   c. What is more ironic, he never worked on his social skills and diction to be more communicative.

   d. As a result, Luke feels like hitting those interrupting him in their face.

Answer Key

Reading Comprehension

1. B
We can infer an important part of the respiratory system are the lungs. From the passage, "Molecules of oxygen and carbon dioxide are passively exchanged, by diffusion, between the gaseous external environment and the blood. This exchange process occurs in the alveolar region of the lungs." Therefore, one of the primary functions for the respiratory system is the exchange of oxygen and carbon dioxide, and this process occurs in the lungs. We can therefore infer that the lungs are an important part of the respiratory system.

2. C
The process by which molecules of oxygen and carbon dioxide are passively exchanged is diffusion.
This is a definition type question. Scan the passage for references to "oxygen," "carbon dioxide," or "exchanged."

3. A
The organ that plays an important role in gas exchange in amphibians is the skin.
Scan the passage for references to "amphibians," and find the answer.

4. A
The three physiological zones of the respiratory system are Conducting, transitional, respiratory zones.

5. B
This warranty does not cover a product that you have tried to fix yourself. From paragraph two, "This limited warranty does not cover ... any unauthorized disassembly, repair, or modification. "

6. C
ABC Electric could either replace or repair the fan, provided the other conditions are met. ABC Electric has the option to

repair or replace.

7. B
The warranty does not cover a stove damaged in a flood. From the passage, "This limited warranty does not cover any damage to the product from improper installation, accident, abuse, misuse, natural disaster, insufficient or excessive electrical supply, abnormal mechanical or environmental conditions."

A flood is an "abnormal environmental condition," and a natural disaster, so it is not covered.

8. A
A missing part is an example of defective workmanship. This is an error made in the manufacturing process. A defective part is not considered workmanship.

9. A
Low blood sugar occurs both in diabetics and healthy adults.

10. B
None of the statements are the author's opinion.

11. A
The author's purpose is the inform.

12. A
The only statement that is not a detail is, "A doctor can diagnosis this medical condition by asking the patient questions and testing."

13. A
Based on the partial table of contents, this book is most likely about how to answer multiple choice.

14. B
This passage describes the different categories for traditional stories. The other choices are facts from the passage, not the main idea of the passage. The main idea of a passage will always be the most general statement. For example, choice A, Myths, fables, and folktales are not the same thing, and each describes a specific type of story. This is a true state-

ment from the passage, but not the main idea of the passage, since the passage also talks about how some cultures may classify a story as a myth and others as a folktale. The statement, from choice B, Traditional stories can be categorized in different ways by different people, is a more general statement that describes the passage.

15. B
Choice B is the best choice, categories that group traditional stories according to certain characteristics.

Choices A and C are false and can be eliminated right away. Choice D is designed to confuse. Choice D may be true, but it is not mentioned in the passage.

16. D
The best answer is D, traditional stories themselves are a part of the larger category of folklore, which may also include costumes, gestures, and music.

All the other choices are false. Traditional stories are part of the larger category of Folklore, which includes other things, not the other way around.

17. A
There is a distinct difference between a myth and a legend, although both are folktales.

18. B
The time limit for radar detectors is 14 days. Since you made the purchase 15 days ago, you do not qualify for the guarantee.

19. B
Since you made the purchase 10 days ago, you are covered by the guarantee. Since it is an advertised price at a different store, ABC Electric will "beat" the price by 10% of the difference, which is,

500 – 400 = 100 – difference in price

100 X 10% = $10 – 10% of the difference

The advertised lower price is $400. ABC will beat this price by 10% so they will refund $100 + 10 = $110.

20. C
The purpose of this passage is to persuade.

21. B
From the first paragraph, "The segments of the body are organized into three distinctive connected units, a head, a thorax, and an abdomen."

This question tries to confuse 'segments' and 'units.'

22. D
This question tries to confuse. Read the passage carefully to find reference to the number of wings. "...if present in the species, two or four wings."
From this, we can conclude some insects have no wings, (if present ...) some have 2 wings and some have 4 wings.

23. A
The question asks about the abdomen and choices refer to organs in the abdomen. The passage says, "The abdomen also contains most of the digestive, respiratory, ... "

The choices are,

    a. It contains some of the organs.

    b. It is too small for any organs.

    c. It contains all the organs.

    d. None of the above.

Choice A is true, but we need to see if there is better choice before answering. Choice B is not true. Choice C is not true since the relevant sentence says 'most' not 'all.' Choice D can be eliminated since Choice A is true.

Given there is not better choice, Choice A is the best choice answer.

24. A
The author is enjoying the daffodils very much and so we can infer that he is a lover of nature.

25. C
The mood of this poem is happy.   From the last line,

And then my heart with pleasure fills,
And dances with the daffodils.

26. D
Sprightly means happy and full of life. From the lines before and after sprightly, we can see it means happy.

Ten thousand saw I at a glance,
Tossing their heads in sprightly dance.

The waves beside them danced, but they
Out-did the sparkling waves in glee:

27. C
Joyful is the best answer. Happy is a possible answer, but joyful is better. Jocund means jovial, exuberant, light-hearted; merry and in high spirits.   From the poem,

Ten thousand saw I at a glance,
Tossing their heads in sprightly dance.

The waves beside them danced, but they
Out-did the sparkling waves in glee:

28. A
We can infer that blood is responsible for transporting oxygen to the cells.

29. C
Calcium is not contained in blood plasma.

From the passage, "[Blood Plasma] contains dissolved proteins, glucose, mineral ions, hormones, carbon dioxide, platelets and the blood cells themselves."

30. A
The lungs exhale the carbon dioxide after venous blood has been carried from body tissues.

Mathematics

1. B
Total Volume = Volume of large cylinder - Volume of small cylinder

Volume of a cylinder = area of base • height = $\pi r^2 \cdot h$

Total Volume = $(\pi \cdot 12^2 \cdot 10) - (\pi \cdot 6^2 \cdot 5) = 1440\pi - 180\pi$

= 1260π in^3

2. C
We are told that driver B is 20 km/h faster than driver A. So: $V_B = V_A + 20$ where V is the velocity. Also, driver B travelled 480 km 2 hours before driver A. So:

x = 480 km

$t_A - 2 = t_B$ where t is the time. Now we know the relationship between A and B drivers in terms of time and velocity. We need to write an equation only depending on V_A (the speed of driver A) which we are asked to find.

Since distance = velocity•time: $480 = V_A \cdot t_A = V_B \cdot t_B$

$480 = (V_A + 20)(t_A - 2)$

$480 = (V_A + 20)(480/V_A - 2)$

$480 = 480 - 2V_A + 20 \cdot 480/V_A - 40$

$0 = -2V_A + 9600/V_A - 40$ ... Multiplying the equation by V_A eliminates the denominator:

$2V_A^2 + 40V_A - 9600 = 0$ ... Simplifying the equation by 2:

$V_A^2 + 20V_A - 4800 = 0$

$V_{A1,2} = [-20 \pm \sqrt{(400 + 4 \cdot 4800)}] / 2$

$V_{A1,2} = [-20 \pm 140] / 2$

$V_A = [-20 - 140]/2 = -80$ km/h and $V_A = [-20 + 140]/2 = 60$ km/h

We need to check our answers. It is easy to make a table:

t_A	V_A	V_B	t_B	$t_A - t_B$
480/80 = 6	-80	-80 - 20 = -100 B is 20 km/h faster than A. - sign only mentions the direction of the velocity. For magnitude, we need to add -20.	480/100 = 4.8	6 - 4.8 = 1.2 This should be 2!
480/60 = 8	60	60 + 20 = 80	480/80 = 6	8 - 6 = 2 This is correct!

So, V_A = 60 km/h is the only answer satisfying the question.

3. C
1 hour is equal to 3,600 seconds and 1 kilometer is equal to 1000 meters.

Since this train travels 72 kilometers per hour, this means that it covers 72,000 meters in 3,600 seconds.

If it travels 72,000 meters in 3,600 seconds

It travels x meters in 12 seconds

By cross multiplication: x = 72,000 • 12 / 3,600

x = 240 meters

4. A
Let us first mention the money Tony spent: $80

Now we need to find the money Tony earned:

He had 15 dozen eggs = 15•12 = 180 eggs. 16 eggs were broken. So,

Remaining number of eggs that Tony sold = 180 – 16 = 164.

Total amount he earned for selling 164 eggs = 164•0.54 = $88.56.

As a summary, he spent $80 and earned $88.56.

The profit is the difference: 88.56 - 80 = $8.56

Percentage profit is found by proportioning the profit to the money he spent:

$8.56 \cdot 100/80 = 10.7\%$

Checking the answers, we round 10.7 to the nearest whole number: 11%

5. A
If we know the coordinates of two points on a line, we can find the slope (m) with the below formula:

$m = (y_2 - y_1)/(x_2 - x_1)$ where (x_1, y_1) represent the coordinates of one point and (x_2, y_2) the other.

In this question:

$(-9, 6) : x_1 = -9, y_1 = 6$

$(18, -18) : x_2 = 18, y_2 = -18$

Inserting these values into the formula:

$m = (-18 - 6)/(18 - (-9)) = (-24)/(27)$ ... Simplifying by 3:

$m = -8/9$

6. C
This equation has no solution.

$x^2 + 4x + 4 + x^2 - 4x + 4 / (x - 2)(x + 2) = 0$

$2x^2 + 8 / (x - 2)(x + 2) = 0 => 2x^2 + 8 = 0$

$x^2 + 4 = 0$

$x_{1,2} = 0 \pm \sqrt{-4 * 4} / 2$

$x_{1,2} = 0 \pm \sqrt{-16} / 2$

Solution for the square root of -16 is not a real number, so this equation has no solution.

7. D
$3x^3 + 13x^2 - 10$
$5(3x^2 - 2) - x^2(2 - 3x)$
$15x^2 - 10 - 2x^2 + 3x^3$
$3x^3 + 13x^2 - 10$

8. B
Number of absent students = 83 − 72 = 11

Percentage of absent students is found by proportioning the number of absent students to total number of students in the class = 11•100/83 = 13.25

Checking the answers, we round 13.25 to the nearest whole number: 13%

9. B
$-x^4 + 2x^2 - 2x$
$(x^3 + 2)(x^2 - x) - x^5$
$x^5 - x^4 + 2x^2 - 2x - x^5$
$-x^4 + 2x^2 - 2x$

10. B
To simplify the expression, we need to find common factors. We see that both terms contain the term ab^2. So, we can take this term out of each term as a factor:

$9ab^2 + 8ab^2 = (9 + 8)ab^2 = 17ab^2$

11. A
If we know the coordinates of two points on a line, we can find the slope (m) with the below formula:
$m = (y_2 - y_1)/(x_2 - x_1)$ where (x_1, y_1) represent the coordinates of one point and (x_2, y_2) the other.

In this question:

$(-4, y_1) : x_1 = -4, y_1 =$ we will find

$(-8, 7) : x_2 = -8, y_2 = 7$

$m = -7/4$

Inserting these values into the formula:

$-7/4 = (7 - y_1)/(-8 - (-4))$

$-7/4 = (7 - y_1)/(-8 + 4)$

$7/(-4) = (7 - y_1)/(-4)$ ... Simplifying the denominators of both sides by -4:

$7 = 7 - y_1$

$0 = -y_1$

$y_1 = 0$

12. A
$x^2 + 12x - 13 = 0$ ... We try to separate the middle term $12x$ to find common factors with x^2 and -13 separately:

$x^2 + 13x - x - 13 = 0$ ... Here, we see that x is a common factor for x^2 and $13x$, and -1 is a common factor for $-x$ and -13:

$x(x + 13) - 1(x + 13) = 0$ ... Here, we have x times $x + 13$ and -1 times $x + 13$ summed up. This means that we have $x - 1$ times $x + 13$:

$(x - 1)(x + 13) = 0$

This is true when either or, both of the expressions in the parenthesis are equal to zero:

$x - 1 = 0$ ... $x = 1$

$x + 13 = 0$ ... $x = -13$

1 and -13 are the solutions for this quadratic equation.

13. D
To find the total turnout in all three polling stations, we need to proportion the number of voters to the number of all registered voters.
Number of total voters = 945 + 860 + 1210 = 3015

Number of total registered voters = 1270 + 1050 + 1440 = 3760

Percentage turnout over all three polling stations = 3015•100/3760 = 80.19%

Checking the answers, we round 80.19 to the nearest whole number: 80%

14. D
Area of Type B consists of two rectangles and a half circle. We can find these three areas and sum them up to find the total area:

Area of the left rectangle: $(4 + 8) \cdot 8 = 96 \text{ m}^2$

Area of the right rectangle: $14 \cdot 8 = 112 \text{ m}^2$

The diameter of the circle is equal to 14 m. So, the radius is $14/2 = 7$:

Area of the half circle = $(1/2) \cdot \pi r^2 = (1/2) \cdot (22/7) \cdot (7)^2 = (1 \cdot 22 \cdot 49)/(2 \cdot 7) = 77 \text{ m}^2$

Area of Type B = $96 + 112 + 77 = 285 \text{ m}^2$

Converting this area to ft²: $285 \text{ m}^2 = 285 \cdot 10.76 \text{ ft}^2 = 3066.6 \text{ ft}^2$

Type B is ($3066.6 - 1300 = 1766.6 \text{ ft}^2$) 1766.6 ft^2 larger than type A.

15. C
First add all the numbers $1 + 2 + 3 + 4 + 5 + 6 + 7 + 8 + 9 + 10 = 55$. Then divide by 10 (the number of data provided) = $55/5 = 11$

16. A
$(a + 2)x - b = -2 + (a + b)x$
$ax + 2x - b = -2 + ax + bx$
$ax + 2x - ax - bx = -2 + b$
$2x - bx = -2 + b$
$(2 - b)x = -(2 - b)$
$x = -(2 - b) : (2 - b)$
$x = -1$

17. D
The area of a rectangle is found by multiplying the width to the length. If we call these sides with "a" and "b"; the area is = $a \cdot b$.

We are given that $a \cdot b = 20 \text{ cm}^2$ ... Equation I

One side is increased by 1 and the other by 2 cm. So new side lengths are "a + 1" and "b + 2."

The new area is $(a + 1)(b + 2) = 35 \text{ cm}^2$ ... Equation II

Using equations I and II, we can find a and b:

$ab = 20$

$(a + 1)(b + 2) = 35$ ... We need to distribute the terms in parenthesis:

$ab + 2a + b + 2 = 35$

We can insert $ab = 20$ to the above equation:

$20 + 2a + b + 2 = 35$

$2a + b = 35 - 2 - 20$

$2a + b = 13$ ... This is one equation with two unknowns. We need to use another information to have two equations with two unknowns which leads us to the solution. We know that $ab = 20$. So, we can use $a = 20/b$:

$2(20/b) + b = 13$

$40/b + b = 13$ ... We equate all denominators to "b" and eliminate it:

$40 + b^2 = 13b$

$b^2 - 13b + 40 = 0$ ... We can use the roots by factoring. We try to separate the middle term $-13b$ to find common factors with b^2 and 40 separately:

$b^2 - 8b - 5b + 40 = 0$ ... Here, we see that b is a common factor for b^2 and $-8b$, and -5 is a common factor for $-5b$ and 40:

$b(b - 8) - 5(b - 8) = 0$ Here, we have b times $b - 8$ and -5 times $b - 8$ summed up. This means that we have $b - 5$ times $b - 8$:

$(b - 5)(b - 8) = 0$

This is true when either or both of the expressions in the parenthesis are equal to zero:

$b - 5 = 0$ ... $b = 5$

$b - 8 = 0$ ... $b = 8$

So we have two values for b which means we have two values for a as well. To find a, we can use any equation we have. Let us use $a = 20/b$.

If $b = 5$, $a = 20/b$ → $a = 4$

If $b = 8$, $a = 20/b$ → $a = 2.5$

So, (a, b) pairs for the sides of the original rectangle are: (4, 5) and (2.5, 8). These are found in (b) and (c) answer choices.

18. D
First add all the numbers 62 + 18 + 39 + 13 + 16 + 37 + 25 = 210. Then divide by 7 (the number of data provided) = 210/7 = 30.

19. B
Based on this graph, a person that is 85 or older will make 31.3 visits to the hospital every year.

20. A
Based on this graph, the number of visits per year is going up as age goes up, so we can expect a person that is 95 to have more than 31.3 visits to the hospital each year.

21. A
The formula of the volume of cylinder is the base area multiplied by the height. As the formula:

Volume of a cylinder = $\pi r^2 h$. Where π is 3.142, r is radius of the cross sectional area, and h is the height.

We know that the diameter is 5 meters, so the radius is 5/2 = 2.5 meters.

The volume is: V = 3.142•2.5²•12 = 235.65 m³.

22. D
1/4x - 2 = 5/6
1 = 5 (4x - 2)/6
6 = 5(4x - 2)
6 = 20x - 10
-20x = -10 - -6
-20x = -16
x = -16/-20 = 0.8

23. C
The large cube is made up of 8 smaller cubes with 5 cm sides. The volume of a cube is found by the third power of the length of one side.
Volume of the large cube = Volume of the small cube•8

= $(5^3)•8 = 125•8$

= 1000 cm^3

There is another solution for this question. Find the side length of the large cube. There are two cubes rows with 5 cm length for each. So, one side of the large cube is 10 cm.

The volume of this large cube is equal to $10^3 = 1000 \text{ cm}^3$

24. A
The line is pointing towards numbers greater than 2. The equation is therefore, X < 2.

25. C
Pythagorean Theorem:
$(\text{Hypotenuse})^2 = (\text{Perpendicular})^2 + (\text{Base})^2$
$h^2 = a^2 + b^2$

Given: a = 6, h = 10
$h^2 = a^2 + b^2$
$b^2 = h^2 - a^2$
$b^2 = 10^2 + 6^2$
$b^2 = 100 - 36$
$b^2 = 64$
$b = 8$

26. A
$(0, -\sqrt{5})$

$y = x\sqrt{5} - \sqrt{5}$
$x - (x\sqrt{5} - \sqrt{5})\sqrt{5} = 5$
$x - 5x + 5 = 5$
$-4x = 5 - 5$
$-4x = 0$

$y = x\sqrt{5} - \sqrt{5}$
$y = 0\sqrt{5} - \sqrt{5}$
$y = \sqrt{5}$

27. C
$-2x^4 - 3x^3 + x^2 - 7x$
$A + B - C = (-2x^4 + x^2 - 3x) + (x^4 - x^3 + 5) - (x^4 + 2x^3 + 4x + 5)$
$-2x^4 + x^2 - 3x + x^4 - x^3 + 5 - x^4 - 2x^3 - 4x - 5$

$-2x^4 - 3x^3 + x^2 - 7x$

Remove the brackets, but change all signs in the third polynomial because of the minus sign. Now group the variables by degrees.

28. D
First arrange the numbers in a numerical sequence - 1,2,3,4,5,6,7,8,9, 10. Then find the middle number or numbers. The middle numbers are 5 and 6. The median = 5 + 6/2 = 11/2 = 5.5

29. D
The decimal point moves 5 places left to be placed after 2, which is the first non-zero number. Thus its 2.011 x 10^{-5} The answer is in the negative because the decimal moved left

30. D
As shown in the figure, two parallel lines intersecting with a third line with angle of 75°.

x = 75° (corresponding angles)

x + y = 180° (supplementary angles) ... inserting the value of x here:

y = 180° - 75°
y = 105°

31. C
$(25/9)^2 = 758/81$

32. D
Two parallel lines (m & side AB) intersected by side AC. This means that 50° and a angles are interior angles. So:
a = 50° (interior angles).

33. A
First arrange the numbers in a numerical sequence - 29,100, 200, 300, 450, 1029, 2001. Next find the middle number. The median = 300.

34. C
$84/231 = 12/33 > 1/3$
$6/35 = 1/5 < 1/3$
$3/22 = 1/7 < 1/3$

35. B
$\sqrt{2}$ is the largest number.
Here are the choices:

    a. 1
    b. $\sqrt{2} = 1.414$
    c. $3/22 = .1563$
    d. $4/3 = 1.33$

36. D
Remove parenthesis
$4Y^3 - 2Y^2 + 7Y^2 + 3Y - Y =$
add and subtract like terms, $4Y^3 + 5Y^2 + 2Y$

37. D
To simplify the expression, remove the parenthesis by distributing the related factors to the terms inside the parenthesis:

$7(2y + 8) + 1 - 4(y + 5) = (7\bullet 2y + 7\bullet 8) + 1 - (4\bullet y + 4\bullet 5)$

$= 14y + 56 + 1 - 4y - 20$

$= 14y - 4y + 56 + 1 - 20$ ... similar terms written together to ease summing/substituting.

$= 10y + 37$

38. D
The distance between two points is found by $= [(x_2 - x_1)^2 + (y_2 - y_1)^2]^{1/2}$

In this question:

$(18, 12) : x_1 = 18, y_1 = 12$

$(9, -6) : x_2 = 9, y_2 = -6$

Distance $= [(9 - 18)^2 + (-6 - 12)^2]^{1/2}$

$= [(-9)^2 + (-18)^2]^{1/2}$

$= (9^2 + 2^2 \cdot 9^2)^{1/2}$

$= (9^2(1 + 5))^{1/2}$ ... We can take 9 out of the square root:

$= 9 \cdot 6^{1/2}$

$= 9\sqrt{6}$

$= 9 \cdot 2.45$

$= 22.04$

The distance is about 22 units.

39. D
We have a circle given with diameter 8 cm and a square located within the circle. We are asked to find the area of the circle for which we only need to know the length of the radius that is the half of the diameter.
Area of circle = πr^2 ... r = 8/2 = 4 cm

Area of circle = $\pi \cdot 4^2$

= 16π cm² ... As we notice, the inner square has no role in this question.

40. B
Perimeter of a parallelogram is the sum of the sides.

Perimeter = 2(l + b)
Perimeter = 2(3 + 10), 2 x 13
Perimeter = 26 cm.

41. D
We understand that each of the n employees earn s amount of salary weekly. This means that one employee earns s salary weekly. So; Richard has ns amount of money to employ n employees for a week.

We are asked to find the number of days n employees can be employed with x amount of money. We can do simple direct proportion:

If Richard can employ n employees for 7 days with ns amount of money,

Richard can employ n employees for y days with x amount

of money ... y is the number of days we need to find.

We can do cross multiplication:

y = (x•7)/(ns)

y = 7x/ns

42. A
Simply find the most recurring number. The most occurring number in the series is 15.

43. B
1 inch on map = 100,000 inches on ground. So 3 inches on map = 3 x 100,000 = 300,000 inches on ground.

44. A
465,890 - 456,890 = 9,000.

45. D
The jacket costs $545.00 so we can round up to $550. 10% of $550 is 55. We can round down to $50, which is easier to work with. $550 - $50 is $500. The jacket will cost about $500.

The actual cost will be 10% X 545 = $54.50
545 – 54.50 = $490.50

46. B
If we know the coordinates of two points on a line, we can find the slope (m) with the below formula:
m = $(y_2 - y_1)/(x_2 - x_1)$ where (x_1, y_1) represent the coordinates of one point and (x_2, y_2) the other.

In this question:

(-4, -4) : x_1 = -4, y_1 = -4

(-1, 2) : x_2 = -1, y_2 = 2

Inserting these values into the formula:

m = (2 - (-4))/(-1 - (-4)) = (2 + 4)/(-1 + 4) = 6/3 ... Simplifying by 3:

m = 2

47. D
The decimal point moves 2 spaces right to be placed after 2, which is the first non-zero number. Thus it is 2.04 x 10^2

48. C
We see that two legs of a right triangle form by Peter's movements and we are asked to find the length of the hypotenuse. We use the Pythagorean Theorem:

$(Hypotenuse)^2 = (Perpendicular)^2 + (Base)^2$
$h^2 = a^2 + b^2$

Given: $3^2 + 4^2 = h^2$
$h^2 = 9 + 16$
$h = \sqrt{25}$
$h = 5$

49. B
Flat Screen TVs are the third best-selling product.

50. B
The two products that are closest in the number of sales, are Flat Screen TVs and Radar Detectors.

English Grammar and Usage

1. D
The preposition "to" is correct. 'To' here means give.

2. A
"Lie" means to recline, and does not take an object. "lay" means to place and does take an object.

3. A
Past unreal conditional. Takes the form,
[If ... Past Perfect ..., ... would have + past participle ...]

4. B
This sentence is in the present tense, so "to find" is correct.

5. A
Always use the singular verb form for nouns like politics, wages, mathematics, innings, news, advice, summons, furniture, information, poetry, machinery, vacation, scenery etc.

6. D
When talking about something that didn't happen in the past, use the past perfect (if I had done).

7. C
"Lie" means to recline, and does not take an object. "Lay" means to place and does take an object. Peter lay the books on the table (the books are the direct object), or the telephone poles were lying on the road (no direct object).

8. C
If one subject linked by "either," "or,""nor" or "neither" is in plural form, then the verb should also be in plural, and the verb should be close to the plural subject.

9. B
"Ran well" is correct. "Ran good" is never correct.

10. D
Both A and C are correct.

> a. Their only employee with a nose ring is a young man named Daniel.
>
> c. Their only employee is a young man with a nose ring named Daniel.

11. C
Use a singular verb with either, each, neither, everyone and many.

12. C
Nouns like deer, sheep, swine, salmon etc can take a singular or plural verb depending if they are used in their singular or plural form.

13. B
The sentence refers to a person, so "who" is the only correct choice.

14. C
The superlative, "hottest," is used when expressing a temperature greater than that of anything to which it is being compared.

15. C
The simple present tense, "rises," is correct.

Essay Revision

1. B
Sentence 4 is a fragment. "Not to mention resolving the conflicts between warring nations."
This sentence is a verbal phrase of the word "resolve" which does not have a main clause as part of the sentence. It is the extension of the sentence preceding it which contains the main clause and does make sense as it stands after the sentence with the main clause. However, since it does not have the main clause in its own structure, it is a sentence fragment.

2. A
The following changes to sentence 6 would focus attention on the main idea in paragraph 2. "Yet, the technology behind the atom bomb had the power of resolving the war itself which scientists like him failed to convey."

The use of the connector "No matter what" in the original sentence is irrelevant given the sense expressed in both the sentences it connects. Taking the context of paragraph into consideration, the use of the connector "Yet" complements the sense expressed in both the sentences.

3. B
Suggested changes for sentence 5, "For example, the atom bomb was developed during the Second World War by the recommendations of the great Albert Einstein - who is accepted as the father of modern physics - in fear of the Germans developing it and using on the Allies."

The original sentence lacks a comma after the thought

extension phrase "for instance," which is replaced with "for example." Also, the use of dash to link two or more ideas and make a point has been incomplete.

4. C
The following sentence, if inserted before sentence 7, would best illustrate the main idea of the passage, "Nuclear fission that is used in the fuelling of the bomb, has the capacity to produce electrical energy which has turned out to be a major alternative later in the Twentieth Century."

The main idea of the passage is the misuse of science regarding the development of the atom bomb during the Second World War, whereas it could effectively be used in meeting the energy demands of the countries involved in the war. This is expressed explicitly in the sentence offered in choice C, which is at the same time coherent with the seventh and eighth sentence between which it is being suggested to be placed. Other choices either lack coherence or are less relevant.

5. C
Sentence 4 is the least relevant to the main idea. "Height concerns also effect routine citizenship privileges such as driving licenses, which require a height of at least 157 cm to be eligible for taking the test in some places."

The first paragraph discusses height discrimination in the job market, but sentence 4 has driving tests as its subject.

6. A
Sentence 3 is not consistent with the author's purpose. "For example, for an air stewardess position, girls have to be no more than 163 cm tall; whereas for jobs in foreign affairs, Chinese diplomats are required to match their foreign counterparts."

The passage talks about the people who want to increase their height by undergoing a surgery and points out the minimum height requirements for getting a job that they wish to work in. However, the expression "no more than 163 cm tall" is a statement about a maximum not a minimum. In addition, the sentence refers to Chinese diplomats who must 'match' the height of their foreign counterparts, which could be taller, and hence require surgery, or could be shorter and not require surgery.

7. B
The following sentence, if inserted after sentence 7, would best illustrate the main idea of the passage, "This artificial way of gaining height is turning out to be a new trend among the new generation in height conscious China."

The paragraph discusses about the application of leg surgery among Chinese young people to increase their height. This is best reflected in the sentence suggested in choice B which also contributes to the cohesion of the second paragraph as well as allowing a smooth transition between the second and third paragraph.

8. B
Suggested changes to sentence 8, "Even parents approve of the idea, being fully aware of all the complications and they are willing to finance such a sophisticated surgery."

The vocabulary usage is incorrect in this sentence. The word "complexity" is an adjective noun used to describe detailed aspects of a given subject which is less relevant here. The word "labyrinth" is also incorrect in this context. The correct counterpart for "complexity" here would be "complications" which takes into account the length of the surgery itself and the agony, sacrifice and the commitment associated with it, all in one. Also the word "sophisticated," as suggested in choices B and C in the place of "labyrinth" is more appropriate as it hints about the details of the surgery.

9. A
Sentence 4 is a fragment. "Which I doubt belongs to any other person."

This sentence is an extension of the sentence preceding it. It does not complete the thought when alone and is thus a sentence fragment.

10. D
Sentence 9 is the least relevant to the main idea of the sec-

ond paragraph. "He is panicked by street dogs and neighbors' cats and to avoid them, he crosses to the other side of the street every now and then."

The second paragraph mainly talks about Luke's odd behavior while in a moving in a crowd, but sentence 9 shifts the subject to his strategy when he encounters cats and dog in the streets.

11. C
Sentence 4 contains a redundant phrase. "Which I doubt belongs to any other person other than him."

In this sentence the second "other" is redundant and can be omitted.

12. B
The following sentence, if inserted before sentence 1, would best illustrate the main idea of the passage. "But that does not bother him; rather he always seems to be happy in being able to utter those two words."

Conclusion

CONGRATULATIONS! You have made it this far because you have applied yourself diligently to practicing for the exam and no doubt improved your potential score considerably! Getting into a good school is a huge step in a journey that might be challenging at times but will be many times more rewarding and fulfilling. That is why being prepared is so important.

Good Luck!

FREE Ebook Version

Download a FREE Ebook version of the publication!

Suitable for tablets, iPad, iPhone, or any smart phone.

Go to
http://tinyurl.com/q25bkez

CAHSEE Test Strategy!

Learn to increase your score using time-tested secrets for answering multiple choice questions!

This practice book has everything you need to know about answering multiple choice questions on the CHSPE!

You will learn 12 strategies for answering multiple choice questions and then practice each strategy with over 45 reading comprehension multiple choice questions, with extensive commentary from exam experts!

Also included are strategies and practice questions for basic math, plus math tips, tricks and shortcuts!

Maybe you have read this kind of thing before, and maybe feel you don't need it, and you are not sure if you are going to buy this Book.

Remember though, it only a few percentage points divide the PASS from the FAIL students.

Even if our multiple choice strategies increase your score by a few percentage points, isn't that worth it?

https://www.createspace.com/4078118

Enter Code GG65A5BY for 25% off!

Get Organized, Study Less and Get Higher Marks!

Here is what you will learn:

- How to Organize your Study Space

- Four different strategies for taking notes - Taking notes is a critical skill for success. Sample lectures with example notes in 4 different styles, with complete explanation and exercises.

- Reading strategies for textbooks, essays, novels and literature

- How to Concentrate - What is concentration and how do you do it!

- Using Flash Cards - Complete guide to using flash cards including the Leitner method.

and LOT more... Including time management, sleep, nutrition, motivation, brain food, procrastination, study schedules and more!

https://www.createspace.com/4060298

Enter Code LYFZGQB5 for 25% off!

Endnotes

Reading Comprehension passages where noted below are used under the Creative Commons Attribution-ShareAlike 3.0 License

http://en.wikipedia.org/wiki/Wikipedia:Text_of_Creative_Commons_Attribution-ShareAlike_3.0_Unported_License

[1] Immune System. In *Wikipedia*. Retrieved November 12, 2010 from, en.wikipedia.org/wiki/Immune_system.
[2] White Blood Cell. In *Wikipedia*. Retrieved November 12, 2010 from en.wikipedia.org/wiki/White_blood_cell.
[3] Infectious disease. In *Wikipedia*. Retrieved November 12, 2010 from http://en.wikipedia.org/wiki/Infectious_disease.
[4] Thunderstorm. In *Wikipedia*. Retrieved November 12, 2010 from en.wikipedia.org/wiki/Thunderstorm.
[5] Meteorology. In *Wikipedia*. Retrieved November 12, 2010 from en.wikipedia.org/wiki/Outline_of_meteorology.
[6] Cloud. In *Wikipedia*. Retrieved November 12, 2010 from http://en.wikipedia.org/wiki/Clouds.
[7] U.S. Navy Seal. In *Wikipedia*. Retrieved November 12, 2010 from en.wikipedia.org/wiki/United_States_Navy_SEALs.
[8] Respiratory System. In *Wikipedia*. Retrieved November 12, 2010 from en.wikipedia.org/wiki/Respiratory_system.
[9] Mythology. In *Wikipedia*. Retrieved November 12, 2010 from en.wikipedia.org/wiki/Mythology.
[10] Insect. In *Wikipedia*. Retrieved November 12, 2010 from en.wikipedia.org/wiki/Insect.
[11] Blood. In Wikipedia. Retrieved November 12,2010 from http://en.wikipedia.org/wiki/Blood.

www.ingramcontent.com/pod-product-compliance
Lightning Source LLC
Chambersburg PA
CBHW070335240426
43665CB00045B/2034